BRASS-POUNDERS:

Young Telegraphers of the Civil War

Brass-Pounders

*Young Telegraphers
of the
Civil War*

Alvin F. Harlow

SAGE BOOKS

DENVER

Sage Books are published by

Alan Swallow, 2679 South York, Denver 10, Colorado

Table of Contents

Illustrations for *Brass-Pounders*
came from F. T. Miller, *Photographic
History of the Civil War,*
Patriot Publishing Co., Springfield, Mass., 1911,
Sparks from the Camp Fire, ed. Joseph W.
Morton, Jr., Keystone Publishing Co.,
Philadelphia, 1892,
and John Emmet O'Brien, *Telegraphing
in Battle,* Scranton, Pa., 1910.

Table of Illustrations

Thanks are due Don Bloch of Denver
for handling the manuscript and
for aid in locating the
illustrations of this book.

I

Overture and Variations

Marion Kerner was there at the overture, the curtain-raiser of the Civil War, a year and a half before it began, though he didn't recognize it at the time. In the autumn of 1859 young Kerner, a blonde Pennsylvanian in his middle teens, was night operator for the Baltimore & Ohio Railroad at Martinsburg, in the extreme northeastern corner of what is now West Virginia, but was then still a part of Virginia.

About an hour and a half past midnight of October 16th-17th Marion was killing time between trains with a tattered copy of a story paper, the New York *Ledger,* meanwhile listening with one ear, operator-fashion, to the words clicking over the restless wires between station and station and headquarters. Suddenly his attention became fixed, riveted; the key was chattering something startling; the operator at Harper's Ferry, 18 miles east of him, was calling the division superintendent's office at Cumberland, 72 miles west of him—calling excitedly, letters tumbling over each other, as if the operator were trying to shout by wire. He butchered his sending badly, but Marion and Cumberland both managed to catch the words;

"Armed men stopped No. 2 here sent all passengers to hotel must have cut wires east of here they ha . . ."

And then, with one final, decisive click, the wire went dead. for several seconds. Finally Cumberland began trying to get Harper's Ferry. "HF, HF, HF" it called insistently, then querulously, but it might as well have been trying to call another world.

It must be explained that No. 2 was the night passenger train eastbound, due at Harper's Ferry at 1:15 A.M., where it must have arrived on time or thereabouts. Harper's Ferry, one of the most picturesquely located towns in the United States, is situated on the south side of the Potomac River, where that stream slashes through the Blue Ridge, and the Shenandoah River joins the Potomac from the south. Rocky heights rise steeply on both sides of both streams, and the town at that time was mostly strung along a narrow bench at the foot of the ridge back of it, with a few buildings straggling up the slope in the rear. A small Government armory, with its workshops, stood on the shelf some forty feet above the river. The B. & O. Railroad, coming eastward on the south side of the Potomac, turns sharply after passing the depot, and crosses to the north shore of the river.

At Cumberland the division superintendent himself was routed out of bed and came grumpily to the office, still skeptical as to the seriousness of the matter, but was convinced when he saw the broken message and found he couldn't get either Harper's Ferry or headquarters at Baltimore on the wire. He called Marion, the nearest night operator to the scene of trouble, and said, "Kerner, do U hear anything about whats up at Harper's Ferry?"

"Not a word," replied Marion, "except that message to U that broke off short. Guess those armed men must have cut the wire just then or slugged the operator."

"Evidently." Cumberland then began again, "HF, HF, HF" but with no more results than before. It was maddening, knowing that something violent, something desperate was going on down there at the Ferry, and no way of finding out what it was. What on earth could it be? Train robbery had not been invented, and the Ferry operator said nothing about molestation of passengers; they had merely been sent to the town hotel, presumably for the remainder of the night, though of course the little hotel couldn't accommodate them all, and it was hard to imagine that any of them could sleep even if they had beds.

A freight train came rumbling into Martinsburg from the west. Marion had put up a red lantern for it, and was telling Cumberland, "Am stopping No. 24 here have U orders for it?" To which Cumberland replied with orders for 24's crew, "Remain at Martinsburg until further orders." It was destined to remain there several days.

At Cumberland the division super said to the operator, "I'll tell you what we'd better do. See if you can get Baltimore by way of Pittsburgh and Philadelphia. Those fellows ought to be willing

10

to help us out when they know that we have an armed insurrection on our line."

It took some doing to get Baltimore, mostly over commercial telegraph lines, but at last within a couple of hours, word came back that Headquarters, too, was in the dark as to the situation at Harper's Ferry. It could get no nearer to that place by wire than Point of Rocks, 13 miles east of there, where there was a night operator. But about 4:30 A.M. another message came from Headquarters, saying that No. 2, with all passengers aboard, had been released shortly after 3 A.M. and was proceeding eastward. And all that Baltimore could get from the crew was the preposterous statement that the raiders were Abolitionists, who were going to free all the slaves in the South! At least, so they said. It just didn't make sense.

As soon as he had stopped the freight train, Marion sent one of the brakemen to the local railroad agent's home to awaken him and tell him of the crisis. He soon hurried to the depot, and had scarcely arrived when he was greeted with a telegram from the division superintendent which read:

"Send someone on hand car as near to Harper's Ferry
as feasible to get news. Get whole story."

Mr. Bridges, the agent, pondered the message for a moment, then looked up at Marion with a whimsical grin.

"Well, Mary," said he (Marion hated that feminine shortening of his name, but he had grown accustomed to it). "It looks as if you're elected."

Marion quickly caught the implication. "You mean—me—go to the Ferry?" he asked in some consternation.

"Yes. You can do it as well as anybody. You'll have to go and wake up Tom McGahan, get him to rout out two or three of his men and take you over there on a hand-car. I'll give you a note to him. Bill" (the day operator) "can take over here. You know where the section shanties are, don't you?"

He did. "Better take your overcoat and a muffler," warned the agent. "It'll be cold riding on that car."

He sent the freight train fireman after Bill, and Marion prepared for his journey. After the first shock had passed, his boyish spirit was rather attracted to the adventure; he thought it might be good fun. "Here's a half-dollar for food," said Mr. Bridges. "You may be at the Ferry for breakfast. Now, don't get

11

into any trouble. Better stop the car outside of town and walk in. You ain't a railroader, remember. Play greenhorn. Just gawp around and ask questions. And here—better wear this old cap. Mustn't look too dressed up."

The old felt farm cap, with a section that pulled down over the ears, had been hung on the wall and left there by a former operator who used it when he went out in stormy weather. Mr. Bridges whacked it against the table a time or two to knock out the dust, and Marion donned it. He was not a very dressy chap at best, and that cap made him look considerably more countrified.

"What in thunder are Bill and that fireman up to?" wondered Mr. Bridges. "I gave him careful instructions just how to reach Bill's home. He couldn't go wrong." Nevertheless, he had gone wrong, and before reaching Bill's place, had awakened two other families who hadn't the slightest interest in him or Bill or the railroad. Bill finally showed up, yawning and grouchy, and Marion set forth on his trek towards the section shanties, about a mile east of town. He followed streets for a while, then took to the railroad track, which wasn't too easy walking in a night lighted only by the stars.

At the section-end, he hammered on the door of Tom McGahan, the section boss, until the latter roared out at him to go away or he would shoot through the door. When finally convinced that the caller came on official business, the big Irishman lighted a candle and came to the door in his underwear. He plodded slowly through the agent's note, grumbling objurgations through his mustache. Marion added what he knew about the episode.

"Hell of a note!" growled McGahan at length, whacking the paper with his hand. "Git up in the small o' the night and pump the car nigh forty mile." He read the note again and hesitated as if questioning whether he would obey the injunction or not. "Bridges ain't my boss," he rumbled.

"No, but the division superintendent is," Marion reminded him. "He distinctly said a hand-car was to be sent to the Ferry to find what's going on."

"Will you bear a hand wit' the handles?" demanded the boss. "Ain't room on the car for five."

Marion had a feeling that McGahan was becoming rather interested in the adventure. "Sure, I'll pull my weight," he agreed.

Without another word McGahan turned to dress himself, telling

12

his wife to prepare a package of bread and meat for his breakfast. Then he visited two neighboring shacks to awaken two of his men. "And fix some lunch for yer breakfasts," he advised.

It was quite some time before they were all assembled, and Tom called to Marion, "Hey, boy help git th' ca-ar on th' thrack."

It was the old-fashioned section crew handcar, now fallen into disuse. Four men stood on its platform in pairs, facing each other, and pumped handles up and down, which worked like an old steamboat walking beam to propel the vehicle. Marion was shivering a little from cold and excitement when they started, but after dropping into the vale of Opequon Creek, the climb up the grade on the other side soon warmed his blood.

"We'll have to take a chance on meetin' a thrain," said McGahan.

"There won't be any trains, I'm sure," said Marion.

They leveled out on a plateau, where for several miles but little effort was needed. Two or three tiny villages were darkly visible as they tooled through them; all soundly asleep—they saw only two dimly lighted windows in more than an hour.

"I helped build this road," mused McGahan, "but I ain't been over it in fifteen or twenty years. I'll be glad to see it again goin' back."

Now they began coasting down a long, gentle slope. "Seddown on th' edge of the ca-ar and rest, boy," said the boss. "Only keep your head down, away from t' handle, and keep yer feet from draggin'." He began applying a brake. "Goin, down towards th' Potowmick," he explained. "This'll be a long, stiff pull comin' back."

The east grew rosy, and slowly the landscape around them took form. "The river's right over there," explained McGahan, gesturing towards his left. "Ah, here's a section." He braked the car to a stop.

It was a little after six, and the section crew were turning out for their day's work. They stared in amazement at sight of a strange hand-car.

"Ahoy, there!" hailed McGahan. "How far would it be to Harper's Ferry?"

"'Bout a mile and three-quarters," was the reply. "Where do yez come from?"

"Martinsburg. We come down here to find out what th'hell the ruckus is at the Ferry."

13

This crew hadn't heard that there was any trouble. The town was around a shoulder of the hill from them, and though there had been some shots fired during the night and at least one man killed, they had heard nothing.

"So we have to come all t' way from Martinsburg to give yez the news about yer own back yard," joked McGahan. He and Marion briefed the startled crew as far as their knowledge went.

"Now," said Mac, to the other boss, "suppose you take this young gossoon about a mile furder on your car, or not so far if you see any sojers. He has gotta find out th' news. I'd take him, only it might look queer to people to see a strange section gang in town. I wudn't advise ye to go into town, for they seem to be makin' railroad men prisoners. Bud, here, is gointa play like a farm boy. Here, son," he opened his package, "take this slice of bread and meat and eat it while ye ride. It'll be probly be th' only breakfast ye'll git. Now jist stroll in there like you didn't know nothin' at all; but don't take any chances."

"If I'm not back in three hours," said Marion, "you'd better go back to Martinsburg."

McGahan made no direct reply to this, having resolved that if the youth did not return within a reasonable time, he would go into town and see what could be done about rescuing him. Marion was dropped from the other crew's hand-car where the adjacent wagon road began to look more like a town street. There was a queasy feeling in his stomach as he saw the car roll away again, and then turned to face the strangely quiet street, where there were no vehicles and few pedestrians. Three of the latter whom he saw were hurrying into their homes, popping inside and slamming the doors. One citizen, approaching his home at a pace slightly less rapid than the others, hurried into his yard and was about to enter the house. Marion hailed him in a guarded tone, "Mister! Oh, Mister!"

The man paused and glanced at him. Wide-eyed, with the old felt cap pulled down partly over his ears, hands jammed into his breeches pockets, pushing back the skirt of his worn overcoat to flap behind him, Marion was a reasonably good representation of a country boy.

"I heard there was some trouble in town," said he. "What is it?"

The citizen cast a quick glance backward over his shoulder

14

towards the town. "Gang of crack-brained Abolitionists have taken over the place," he said. "Came across the river last night."

"What for?"

"Say they're going to free all the slaves in the South."

"How many of 'em are there?"

"Can't tell. Forty or fifty, maybe." (Actually, there were no more than twenty-two.) "Been hiding in the Maryland hills for days. Led by an old fellow, about sixty, named Brown. Tough old cooster. He killed some Democrats in Kansas years ago—shot 'em down in cold blood, and thought he was doing a righteous act."

"But how's he gointa free the slaves?"

"Thinks he'll start an uprising among 'em all over the South. They'll kill their masters, and then they'll be free. He's grabbing citizens of this town, shutting 'em up in the Armory and says the ransom for each of 'em will be one nigger slave."

"Must be crazy."

"Crazy as a bedbug. I haven't seen him, but they say his eyes glitter like a cornered catamount's."

Marion felt that this stranger could be trusted, so he revealed his identity and told why he was there.

"I'm told they released that captured train," said the citizen, "about three o'clock this morning; sent it away with all the passengers on it, I understand. I don't know why, unless old Brown just didn't want to be bothered with it or the passengers."

He continued to glance back uneasily, and was evidently anxious to get out of sight, but Marion asked one more question;

"Isn't there any chance to get help?"

"A man rode over to Charles Town, the county seat, about nine miles from here, three or four hours ago. Had to rowst the county officials out of bed. They talked of calling out the militia. Well, good-day, son. You can bet I'm not opening my store today. I'm staying home. You better go back to Martinsburg."

He bolted into his house and shut the door. Marion decided to risk entering the town; he hoped the raiders wouldn't regard a rustic teen-ager as being of much consequence. He sauntered on, trying to look as countrified as he could. Presently he sighted a man with a gun at a street corner; seedy in attire, with a blanket draped around him, evidently in lieu of an overcoat. Marion stared at him, approached and asked "Are you a soldier?"

"I am one of the Liberators," was the prideful reply.

15

His questioner seemed to ponder this a moment, then asked, "Liberator of what?"

"Of all the colored slaves in Ameriky."

"How you gointa do it?"

"Encourage 'em to rise and strike off their chains."

"Are there Liberators anywhere else besides here?" was the next question.

The sentry's eyes shifted uneasily as he replied, "That ain't none of your business."

This is the only place, thought Marion. His amazement at the foolhardiness of the move increased. He turned away.

"Better be keerful how you sashay around," warned the sentry. "You might git took up or git hurt."

"I'll be keerful," agreed Marion as he ambled on, his eyes and ears alert to everything. On a lower level, he saw men tearing up the railroad track near the depot. He saw two "Liberators" hustling a protesting man through the gate of the Armory yard and into the door of the building, giving him a final triumphant shove as he staggered inside. Then he noticed two more fellows— Liberators, no doubt—leading another man towards the gate. And finally, standing beside the gate, studying a paper in his hand and writing something on it, he saw a tall, gaunt man, long-bearded, in worn clothing, apparently in his late fifties. The men passing him addressed him as Captain Brown.

"Watson," said he to one of these men, "order breakfast at the Wager House for forty-five men—side-meat, bread and coffee. We've got to feed these prisoners, as well as our own force. Food for at least twenty-five—maybe more—must be brought here to the Armory."

The man hurried away and Brown's glance fell upon Marion. He had the eager, hawklike face and eyes of a fanatic.

"What are you doing here, boy?" he demanded.

Marion had his answer all ready. "Jist come into town to see what's goin' on," he replied.

"Your pa own any slaves?"

"Shucks, no. Pa says it's all he can do to feed and clothe the family, let alone a passel o' niggers."

"Not a very elevated sentiment," remarked the leader, "but better than nothing."

16

At that moment, two shots were heard somewhere, and a man came running.

"Cap'n, Orby shot a man—a grocer," he quavered. "But he shot at us first."

"God has judged him," said the old man, solemnly. And then, noticing Marion again, "Get away from here, boy! Go back to the country. This is no place for you."

Marion decided that he had seen and heard enough. He started back, along the way he had come, his pace unconsciously growing ever faster as he went. When he was still half a mile from the section house, McGahan sighted him and came to meet him with the hand-car. He told his story to the amazed section gangs, and the local boss decided not to do any more work "until we find out what's what." But McGahan and Company spat on their hands and began the long, hard pull up that grade, some six miles of it. When they had topped it, the boss told Marion to sit down again and rest while the others did the pumping. They were back at Martinsburg, right alongside the station platform, before 11 o'clock, and Marion had to tell the tale not only to the agent, but to an increasing crowd of listeners, over and over again. He ate an early lunch and tumbled into bed, to sleep away the afternoon. Next day he was so stiff and sore from the unaccustomed work that he could scarcely get out of bed, walk, sit down in a chair or rise from it.

And now the shadow of doom was thickening fast over the Liberators at Harper's Ferry; militia was closing in from three directions, and Marines were coming from Washington. Emergency telegraph service established just outside the town chattered in rapid staccato the events of the next day and a half; the encircling of Brown's little band by an overwhelming force, its sturdy, senseless resistance in an engine house, Brown's defeat and capture with the loss by death of two of his sons (a third escaped), the pitiable laceration of his own body by sword-cuts and bayonet-thrusts; and then, a few days later, the preliminary examination and the four-days' trial of the old man for conspiracy, treason and murder, with the injured prisoner lying on a pallet on the floor, his conviction, followed by that of some of his commandos and his execution on December 2d, a cold day when his thin trousers fluttering in the wind as he stood on the scaffold led some spectators to assert that his legs were shaking with fright; a cruel error, for John Brown never knew fear.

17

His own adventure had been a somewhat thrilling one to Marion Kerner at the time; but not until days, weeks and months of great excitement and editorial fury had passed, with Brown as a hero in many Northern pulpits, college halls and editorial sanctums, and the blackest of villians in the South, did he begin to realize the significance of the affair, yet still with wonder. How could it be so important, he questioned; just a stupid attempt by a monomaniac to do something obviously impossible, something which had failed miserably, as it was bound to fail. But as time went on, it appeared that the madcap escapade of the old Abolitionist was destined never to be forgotten in America. Marion became increasingly proud of his "interview" with John Brown and retold it frequently, perhaps, as his years multiplied, embroidering it a little in the telling, as old men are apt to do. During the war which followed soon afterward, his nerves tightened, and he saw again that dull October day in Harper's Ferry when he heard marching Federal soldiers at time crooning a Southern camp meeting song with new words which had sprung mysteriously out of somewhere;—

"John Brown's body lies a-mouldering in the tomb;
John Brown's body lies a-mouldering in the tomb;
John Brown's body lies a-mouldering in the tomb;
His soul is marching on."

And soon a pretty, sprightly, auburn-haired lady in Boston, a Mrs. Julia Ward Howe, wrote a patriotic poem with religious overtones which fitted the tune, and it became the Battle Hymn of the Republic.

II

Andy, the Young Super

Joe Taylor, telegraph operator at Greensburg, Pennsylvania, a county-seat town 30 miles east of Pittsburgh, was chucking some superfluous paper into his office wastebasket one day in 1849, in preparation for a two-weeks absence, when a voice at the door of his little cubicle said inquiringly, "Mr. Taylor?"

"Yes," said Taylor, turning to look at the caller. He saw a boy in his teens, a stocky, broad-faced, ash-blonde youth beaming at him wistfully, wearing a funny little round hat and baggy trousers and carrying a limp, lumpy carpet-bag. He had just stepped off the stagecoach from Pittsburgh; the railroad had not been completed between the two places.

"Andrew Carnegie," said the youngster, introducing himself. "I've come to take your place while you're away."

Taylor could only stare blankly for a moment. They were acquainted by wire, but had never seen each other before.

"I've talked to you many a time," said young Carnegie, "and I—"

"Yes, yes, I know," interrupted Taylor. "Excuse me for being sorta knocked over, Andy. I knew you hadn't been on the job long, but somehow I hadn't expected you to be quite so young."

"I'm nearly 17," defended Andy.

"How nearly?" queried Taylor, laughing.

Andy grinned in turn. "A few months."

"You don't look even that old. Do you think you can handle the job?"

"The chief seems to think so, and that's more important," said Andy. "You've talked to me—heard me send. Don't you think I do pretty well?"

"Darned well," agreed Taylor. "Well, if Mr. Brooks says you'll do, why, you'll do—that's flat."

And so Taylor started on his trip next day, and 16-year-old Andy Carnegie, on his first important assignment, showed the qualities that were to make him a railroad official within a few years, and eventually, America's greatest steel manufacturer.

Boys in those days often went into business at an early age; economic necessity drove many to work rather than to school. Nothing so fascinated them as the telegraph. No sooner was the first wire put into service by Morse than boys' fingers began to itch for the feel of the brass key. Their enthusiasm, devotion and skill were like those of the radio "hams" of today. The difference is that the boys of those days had to have jobs around a telegraph office before they could touch a key, whereas today's ham needs only get a wave-length, set up his outfit, and he's in business. A century ago a boy no sooner became a telegraph messenger than he began practicing on a temporarily idle key in the office, then began calling neighboring towns early in the morning for practice, and presently he was an "op." Numerous railroad presidents began thus, including Sir William Van Horne, chief builder of the Canadian Pacific Railroad and its great steamship and hotel system, who at 15 was a railroad station agent and operator at Joliet, Illinois. In Wisconsin in 1850, when little telegraph companies were scattered all over the map, J. J. S. Wilson at 16 was manager of the new line between Madison and Chicago.

Carnegie soon attracted the attention of Thomas A. Scott, superintendent of the Western Division of the Pennsylvania Railroad—Altoona to Pittsburgh. He became Scott's secretary, then his assistant, and finally, when Scott was elevated to a vice-presidency, Andrew succeeded to his place as division superintendent. He was then just a few days short of his twenty-fourth birthday.

That was in the fall of 1859, a few days after John Brown's raid on Harper's Ferry. The divided Nation was moving steadily towards Civil War. With the Confederate firing on Fort Sumter, in April, 1861, war became a reality. Simon Cameron, the new Secretary of War, summoned Mr. Scott to come to Washington as Assistant Secretary in charge of transportation, and Scott in turn called on his "young reliable," Andy Carnegie, to help him.

Andy faced a tough problem at once. A Massachusetts regiment had been attacked by mobs when passing through Baltimore, four of its men killed and several wounded. Saboteurs had burned some bridges (all wooden then), cut telegraph wires and torn up tracks at places along the railroad from Philadelphia through Baltimore to Washington, really a national life-line. Trainloads of much-needed troops from the North and Northeast were being prevented from reaching Washington. Young Carnegie started driving relentlessly with a force of engineers, carpenters, tracklayers and men from the delayed regiments, pushing the repaired track towards the Capitol. At Havre de Grace, where the railroad crosses the Susquehanna River, the bridge was still standing, but beyond that, there was damage to tracks and wires.

"Mr. Carnegie," said one man who was escorting a bedraggled boy, "here's a telegraph operator that's been a prisoner of the rebels. He can tell you something, maybe."

The operator was a tired, good-looking boy of fifteen, whose torn, muddy clothing and shoes and generally dishevelled appearance indicated that he had been through some strenuous experiences.

"You are an operator for the P.W. & B. Railroad?" asked Carnegie.

"Yes, sir," was the reply. "I was at Back River, six miles this side of Baltimore."

(Back River is one of those little streams—others are Bush and Gunpowder Rivers—which broaden into wide estuaries as they approach Chesapeake Bay.)

"And your name?"

"William J. Dealey," said the boy. "I reckon you heard that a Massachusetts regiment was mobbed in Baltimore a coupla days ago and a lot of its men killed and wounded?"

"Yes, we know that."

"Well, there was a squad of half a dozen railroad men supposed to be guardin' my office," Bill Dealey went on. "The company was tryin' to keep in communication with Baltimore, but the wire into there went dead, and as I was the last office before Baltimore, headquarters kept after me all the time to ask what was going on and what I could find out. But how could I find out anything? Anyhow, I stuck to the key for fifty-six hours without sleep, and finally just couldn't stay awake any longer. Must've been around two o'clock Sunday morning when I passed out. I woke up three

21

or four hours later when the night mail came along, and there was a whole slew of Baltimore police and men with all kinds of guns—not reg'lar soldiers—all around my station. They'd swamped my guard and they took over the train and burned the bridge.

" 'What did you do that for?' I asked one of the policemen.

" 'To keep mobs in Baltimore from bein' stirred up to riot by Yankee troops comin' through,' he says, and he grinned. They'd picked up another operator, Swift, at Magnolia; took us both into Baltimore and held us. Wanted me to join a light artillery company that they said was being organized for the South, but I says, 'No, thank you, I'm just a telegraph operator.' They didn't keep a very close watch on us, so after a while, I just sneaked away; don't know what became of Swift. I followed a wagon road for a ways out of town, then took to the railroad, and walked all the way here—thirty-six miles. They'd tried to burn the draws of the bridges over Bush and Gunpowder Rivers; succeeded at Gunpowder, and I had to steal a skiff there and row across. But at Bush River the fire had only partly burned the draw and went out; wood was wet from rain. I crawled across there on one of the rails—still hanging together, you know—and finally got here." He heaved a sigh. "I sure am tired—and hungry."

"I don't wonder," agreed Carnegie. "Get him some grub and coffee," he told one of his men. "Well, Billy," clapping him on the shoulder, "you sound like just the sort of man we need. Come with us down the road to give us information and help restring the telegraph wire. I'll arrange it with your company. But first fill your skin full of grub and then lie down and have a nap."

Carnegie and his force worked around the clock—he working as hard as anybody—rebuilding track and bridges and restringing wire. They met no interference in going through Baltimore. But to the beleagured Capitol, they seemed dreadfully slow in coming. Confederate soldiers were inching near and nearer, and the food supply actually began to run short in the city; famine was staring it in the face. Nothing could be heard from the railroad builders but an occasional scout who came through on foot or on horseback or by boat down the bay and up the Potomac River. At times the new President, Lincoln, walked the floor, muttering, "Why don't they come? Why don't they come?"

But they were doing their best. At last the track was in fair shape below Baltimore, but they still could not get in touch with

22

Washington by wire. Carnegie was in the cab of the engine drawing the first trainload of troops over the repaired track towards the Capitol—running slowly, not only for fear of possible sabotage to the track, but so that Carnegie could watch the telegraph wire every foot of the way for breaks.. Suddenly he cried to the engineer, "Stop! Stop quick!"

The engineer reversed his locomotive—for there were as yet no air brakes—and they slid to a stop. Carnegie had seen that the wire had been loosed from a couple of poles so that it hung in a long festoon, which had been pinned to the ground at one point by a peg. This would prevent its carrying messages just as effectively as if it had been cut. Andrew sprang from the engine and ran to the grounded wire, which of course had been drawn very tight when it was pinned down. He pulled with both hands at the peg, which had been driven deeply. Suddenly it came loose, the wire whipped upward and struck him across the face, knocking him down and cutting a gash across his cheek. He went into Washington, holding a bloody handkerchief to his face, and later boasted jokingly that he was one of the first to shed his blood for the Union.

In Washington, after having his cheek patched up, he called on the Secretary of War.

"What happened to your face?" Mr. Carmeron wanted to know. "Been in a battle already?"

Andy explained. Their talk was crisp and rapid-fire; everybody was in a hurry in Washington in those days. Presently the Secretary said, with a sly grin, "Now, here's all I want from you, Mr. Carnegie. I've talked to Mr. Scott, and he says you can do it as easy as turning your hand over; an extension of the B. & O. track here in the city! a new ferry and a rebuilt bridge across the Potomac, and some first-class telegraphers—four to begin with; one to get a military telegraph system organized, and three more for duty here in Washington. Can you get them off the Pennsylvania Railroad?"

"I think I can," said Carnegie.

"Write a dispatch for them right now," ordered the Secretary, pushing a sheet of paper at him.

So Andy wrote a message to one of his old Allegheny boyhood chums, Davy McCargo, now superintendent of telegraphs on the Pennsylvania, saying, "Send four of your best operators to Wash-

23

ington at once, prepared to enter Government telegraph service for the war." The Secretary sent it to a telegraph office, and they discussed plans for half an hour. Next morning, dependable David replied:

> Altoona, April 23, 1861
> Message received. Strouse from Mifflin, Brown from Pittsburgh, O'Brien from Greensburg and Bates from Altoona will start from Washington immediately.
>
> David McCargo

Of these four, Strouse, the eldest, was 23, the others ranged in age down to 18.

"Now there's another operator, a loyal boy named Dealey, whom I ran into on the way down," began Andy.

"Put him on rations and keep your finger on him," broke in Cameron. "We'll be needing operators a-plenty right away."

When the four Pennsylvanians arrived and hurried to the War Department, they found an imposing group of higher-ups, headed by Secretary of State Seward, Secretary of War Cameron and General Winfield Scott, assembled to receive them. Topping them all in magnificence, the portly, pompous old General Scott, relic of the War of 1812 and the Mexican War, but still commanding general of the Army, considered himself the ranking expert in military science. Over against the wall, saying little, was a lank character in a plug hat, and it slowly dawned upon the boys that this was President Lincoln.

Of the four newcomers, Strouse, the senior, was ordered to organize the military telegraph system, which at that time was only for the East, and specifically, for the area around Washington. The war was only in its beginning stage, and everybody was just groping his way; nobody could see far into the future. Brown was held in the War Department, O'Brien was sent to a railroad station and Bates to the Navy Yard, where for some reason or other, he was confined to his room on the ground floor, with a sentry pacing a beat which passed directly in front of his door. The reason for this arrangement is a mystery, unless it was that the military mind found it difficult to trust a civilian. After four days of confinement there, with little to do, the boredom became unbearable, and one evening Homer quietly locked his door, slipped out through a window and went uptown, where he strolled around for an hour, observing the turmoil of a troubled, frightened capitol, with war rumblings just outside its gates. When he returned, he made more noise than he had intended in entering his window, and the sentry quickly thundered on his door.

"Look here, young feller," he barked when it was opened (the sentry himself might have been about eighteen), "you been outside this room."

"I just went for a walk uptown," said Homer, meekly.

"Good thing I didn't ketch you climbin' in that winder," said the guard. "I got orders to shoot."

"Shoot a Government telegrapher?" exclaimed Bates, incredulously.

"Shoot anybody goin' in or out this room," was the reply. "Now you stay inside or you'll go outa here in a box."

Bates notified Secretary Cameron by telegraph of his predicament, and the absurd situation was promptly corrected. He was presently transferred to the War Office uptown, where the staff was steadily increasing in number.

Thus began one of the most remarkable of war operations. There had never been anything quite like it before, anywhere. Railroad telegraphers along the border, those who appeared loyal, were informally taken into Government service, often remaining at their stations. Others were brought from other parts of the North to Washington and near-by important posts. One such was Charlie Jacques, a 16-year-old Ohioan, who found himself suddenly planted at Chain Bridge, only five or six miles above Washington, with orders to stay there until death, a company of Johnnies at the other end of the none-too-long bridge, and he, Charlie, with no horse, nothing but his own two legs as means of escape if worst came to worst. He hardly dared sleep for several days; but they never ventured to cross the bridge.

Ed Conway, who came from Canada, was similarly marooned at Point of Rocks, forty miles farther up the Potomac. He was alone in a tiny cottage, and a Confederate post across the river had a cannon, with which they were getting his range more and more accurately. One by one they shot off his front steps, then the porch, and finally most of the roof. At that, Ed thought it was time to evacuate, especially as he now saw soldiers crossing the bridge at the double-quick. He notified the War Department, "Closing my office for repairs," and with his instrument under his arm, dived through a back window into the tall grass and scrub, and made his way towards Washington on foot.

The changes in the Washington war office were so rapid and numerous they were dizzying. David Strouse, who had been set to organize the telegraph service, was frail in health, and the strain of his job was too much for him. He resigned it in a few weeks and died in the following November. He was succeeded briefly by James R. Gilmore, who was not yet of age. Gilmore had to go over into Virginia to get poles—saplings 15 to 18 feet long—for telegraph lines, from Southern-sympathizing farmers who were not keen about letting the Yankee have them; and Jimmy hastily raised a beard to give him a better air of authority in dealing with them.

The need for more experienced men at the top became apparent, and Anson Stager and Thomas T. Eckert, Western Union officials, were drawn into Government service. Having superior posts, they were given army commissions. Stager had general supervision of the telegraph system, while Major Eckert throughout the war managed the Headquarters telegraph office at Washington. There he did some remarkable bits of message-juggling and personal strategy such as would have been possible in no other country than this, but which served to countercheck what would have been disastrous stupidities on the part of higher-ups. Stager devised a cipher which, as developed by his youthful aides, D. Homer Bates, Albert B. Chandler and Charles A. Tinker, became the standard cipher of the army, the first ever used in war, and never cracked by the enemy. Using ordinary words and some proper nouns, a message sent in it seemed like nonsensical gibberish. The cipher was changed a few times when a copy had been lost or was feared captured by the enemy, but the Federal experts always maintained their superiority. On the Confederate side commercial telegraph lines were largely used, and the Southern war department never built a great system of military wires as was done by the North.

The Telegraph Corps was never really a part of the Army. It was simply a civilian bureau, attached to the Quartermaster's department, and as such was scornfully regarded by the military, especially as the majority of the operators around Washington and in the Eastern sector—which was first to be organized—were boys in their teens. Some were so young at the start that when the four years of war were over, they were not yet eligible to vote. Of course, from there the ages ranged on upward.

The Signal Corps, the flag wigwaggers, whose noses were put out of joint by the telegraph, were particularly huffy about the new service, and thought it should be put under their control. Signal Corps officers tried to give orders to telegraph operators now and then, but were usually ignored. A Signal Corps officer, a Major Myer, being in Hampton, Virginia, one day in '61, decided to "inspect" the telegraph service there. He had never been in direct contact with telegraphers before, and it was something of a shock to him to find in the office only two callow boys in shirt-sleeves and bare feet, sitting on the floor, filling in a quiet interval by playing Seven-up wtih a deplorably dirty, greasy pack of cards. They glanced up when he appeared in the door, but did not notice him otherwise.

"Are you the operators here?" demanded the major.

"Yes, sir," said one of the boys.

The major had been swelling and reddening rapidly. "And don't you salute an officer?" he thundered.

"We're not required to, sir," was the reply. "We're not in the Army. We're civilians."

The major stomped out of there, not hearing the muffled snickers behind him, and went back to Washington, firmly convinced that the Army Telegraph wouldn't do, and should be abolished.

It has often been remarked that a large percentage of the Civil War soldiers were teen-agers. The boyish private soldier was not nearly as remarkable as the young telegraph operator, on whose slender shoulders the responsibility was enormous. It may seem incredible today that the safety and strategy of great armies should often have depended upon the courage, loyalty, judgment, accuracy and cool heads of mere boys, but it was so. In their leisure moments they enjoyed play as much as any boys, but when on duty, no one could be more serious, more determined on getting the job done and done well. In the first two years of the war, operators were given no means of transportation except such as they could grab on Army wagons or caissons, carrying their instruments and a small coil of wire with them. Sometimes they just walked.

In the beginning, no military rank was considered, even for top telegraph officials. The men and boys who pounded the keys in offices or in the field, and the linemen who, at the risk of their lives, strung wire, often under heavy fire in great battles, were just employees, poorly paid, and getting little or no official credit for their work. But they stuck to it like leeches, inspired by grit, patriotism and the fascination of the life. If there were any instances of cowardice or neglect of duty among them, we have yet to find them.

When the war broke out, the top brass at Washington had the notion that the privately owned telegraph companies could handle the military telegraph work. But when experts like Tom Scott, Carnegie and General George B. McClellan knocked that idea out of their heads, they were up to their ears in trouble. They had no wire, no insulators, no instruments, no anything. Jimmy Gilmore, then in charge, appealed to E. S. Sanford, head of the American Telegraph Company, which served Washington, to supply the needed equipment, and try to collect the bill for it afterward. Sanford patriotically took a chance, and after a long delay, his company was able to get its money. Gilmore was presently moved elsewhere, and Anson Stager, an older man, an official of the Western Union Telegraph Company, was appointed to the top job. When the Quartermaster-General refused to honor Stager's requisitions for money and supplies, the War Secretary was bullied into making him a colonel and Assistant Quartermaster. He appointed Thomas T. Eckert his assistant with the rank of major, and Eckert really ran the military telegraph throughout the war. Gilmore and nine other department chiefs were made captains, and these were the only commissions handed out to an organization of 1200 men.

Meanwhile, Carnegie, with an augmented force, worked furiously, almost without sleep, rebuilding the old Long Bridge across the Potomac so that heavy trains could cross it—grabbing timbers wherever they could find them—the bridge was all wood, of course—in the unbelievably brief time of eight days; some say a week. Then they turned their attention to the extension of the track in the city. Carnegie's protege, Billy Dealey, was now a Government operator, and having his adventures. He and another boy named Pritchard, being ordered to set up an office at the end of a certain extension into Virginia, reached the place after dark on a chilly, rainy, evening, and finding no nearer base, took possession of a deserted pig-sty, roofing it inadequately with a blanket, and sat there, wet and shivering, under the drip until morning.

The hour of armed conflict was near at hand. General Mc-Clellan, invading the mountains of what was to become West Virginia, an area which leaned away from the Southern cause, took with him the first field telegraph that ever advanced with an American army. In fact, this was the first war in history in which field telegraph was used. McClellan carried wire and insulators with him, and his operator, 18-year-old A. Harper Caldwell, was one of the top telegraph stars of the war, serving for long afterwards as chief operator and cipher expert to the successive commanders of the Army of the Potomac.

From April to mid-November, 1861, there was constructed in the several Federal departments from the Atlantic coast to Missouri, 1137 miles of telegraph line, in addition to what already ran along the railroads. At first, a bare wire was used, so of course there had to be insulators nailed preferably on poles, though on tree-trunks if no limbs or foliage touched the wire. But within a couple of years they were using a wire coated with rubber, which could be draped over boughs, fences, bushes, anything, provided the rubberizing was well done.

But there were still not enough lines. When General Robert Patterson moved with 16,000 troops across the Potomac above Washington in June, 1861, theoretically to keep the Confederate General Johnston busy, he took no telegraph with him, but communicated by courier through the commercial telegraph offices in Hagerstown and Harper's Ferry. General Scott, the aged commander-in-chief, actually lost track of him for a time, and in turn, Patterson lost sight of Johnston. When Patterson notified Washington that he had Joe Johnston pinned down, old Joe was actually well on his way to join Beauregard, commander of the Confederate army, who was digging in along Bull Run, and who was in touch with his capital, Richmond, by railroad telegraph. When Patterson finally notified Washington on July 20th that Johnston had slipped away from him, the news was not even relayed to General Irvin McDowell, who, with 20,000 troops, had been given the job of whipping Beauregard.

When McDowell, with his rabble of raw troops and a few regulars, moved out from Washington to attack Beauregard, Charlie Jacques, brought down from Chain Bridge, was stationed at Springfield, on the railway telegraph behind his army—later moved a few miles forward to Burke's Station—and a branch line was run to Fairfax Court House, McDowell's headquarters there. Mc-Dowell kept in touch with his subordinates along Bull Run by courier, and was expected to wire Washington every 15 minutes.

In the War Department telegraph office that Sunday afternoon, July 21, 1861, a complacent party, including President Lincoln and most of his cabinet, and General Scott, commander-in-chief, and several of his staff, sat waiting for news from what they believed would be the concluding scene of the rebellion, out along Bull Run. Secretary of State Seward, blowing smoke rings from his cigar, had predicted that the war wouldn't last more than thirty days. A number of Congressmen and Government officials had driven out towards the battlefields, some taking their wives and lady friends along in their carriages, to see the fun at close range.

For the first few hours that afternoon, all news was encouraging. Everything was going according to plan; in a short time, all would be over. But as the hot, still summer dusk approached, the clicking of the instrument ceased. A long silence, and then Washington asked Fairfax for news. The reply was, "No courier has arrived from the front for some time." McDowell was covering up, hoping for something better to tell. Again a long wait, again a query both to Fairfax and Burke's, only to get the reply, "No news."

"Guess our men are chasing the Rebels so hard and so fast," surmised someone in the office, "that they're plumb out of reach of the telegraph."

"And haven't time to write messages, anyhow," suggested another.

Dusk deepened. At last the instrument clicked the Washington call, and Bates began to write. A shell from a Confederate gun hurled into their midst could scarcely have created more consternation in the group than did that one fateful sentence, *"Our Army is in full retreat."*

Immediately a chorus of disbelief burst forth: "Oh, that can't be right!" "Something queer!" "Mistake!" "You've got it wrong, young fellow"—

"No, I haven't," Bates maintained, still scribbling. "I couldn't make a mistake on this. Here's more of it." Thereafter the clicker steadily became more rapid, more excited, as bits of reports from officers told of the slaughter, the rout, the jamming of troops,

30

artillery, baggage wagons and Congressmen's carriages in the narrow roads and bridges, the confusion and panic in the gathering darkness. It was a sickening recital, and the Administration found later that the half had not been told. The remnants of the defeated army streamed back towards Washington by wagon roads, by railroad tracks, across country, any way it could find footing. The humiliated commander, General McDowell, and his staff were back in the city late in the night. As his shattered legions stumbled back through the darkness past Charlie Jacques's uneasy post, the young operator asked the War Department, "Shall I come in?"

"Stay where you are," was the gruff reply; and so he stayed while the pitiful pageant went on. Even with the rumblings of retreat around him, the occasional shot or nervous fusillade fired at nothing but some frightening sound, Charlie, worn with his long vigil, nodded over his table; aroused now and then by some colonel, brigadier or surgeon barging into his office to ask, "Aren't there any trains running into the city? No engines that can take cars in, even if it's only freight cars? Are they going to let our wounded lie out here and die or be captured?"

"I'll ask," Charlie would reply, but he never got a definite answer. Chaos, stupefaction, seemed to rule at Headquarters.

"Tell 'em," he was ordered, "that some of our field hospitals were captured by the enemy, but there are hundreds, maybe thousands of wounded men still not prisoners, some in ambulances groping their way along dark roads—and occasionally running over a fallen man—some standing stock still because of darkness, broken bridges, jammed roads . . . and many suffering men lying on the bare ground."

"I'll tell them," said Charlie, hammering the key more industriously, making something of a jumble of the news, but obtaining no better results than before.

Slowly the night hours dragged on. The noise of retreat subsided to a murmur. The whole Union army must have passed me, Charlie thought; any moment now, the Rebels will be here and I'll be a prisoner. But General Beauregard, some thought, had missed a great opportunity that evening in not pressing his advantage, keeping right on the heels of the defeated army into Washington. At length Charlie timidly asked Headquarters, "Shall I close my office?"

"If you leave your post without permission," barked the ticker,

31

"you will be shot." A pretty rough threat to hurl at a boy who had never been so close to a battle before, and who, despite the fact that he was momentarily expecting to be closer still, was sticking to his job. But the War Department's nerves were on edge.

There was one man, however, connected with the Department who had not slept that night, and who, hearing reports from the retreating officers, was worrying about those wounded. Andrew Carnegie finally said to Colonel Tom Scott, "I think we must get those wounded men back here by rail, don't you? There's a shortage of ambulances, as there is of everything else."

"Right," said Colonel Scott. "Get Haupt to do it."

"I'll attend to it myself," said Carnegie, "with Haupt collaborating, of course."

"But be careful; don't run your trains into the enemy's line," warned Scott.

Enlisting the help of Colonel Herman Haupt, a railroad technician, Carnegie had two locomotives fired up and some cars assembled. He himself rode in the engine cab of the first train that moved across Long Bridge and cautiously out to Springfield and Burke's. It was just before dawn—a dawn that was late that day because a slow drizzle had begun falling. It took more than an hour to cover the 20 miles out to Burke's.

"We'll do better when it gets daylight," apologized the engineer. "It's skeery business in the dark; never know when a culvert will be out."

Word of their coming had been wired ahead, and many wounded had been gathered at Burke's—more than a trainload. Others were coming.

"No Reb yet?" asked Carnegie of an officer.

"No, strangely enough, they don't seem to have advanced an inch since yesterday evening. Guess they wore themselves out, licking us."

That trainload of shattered men ambled back to the Capitol, and then came another and another. All through most of that dark day the rescue trains shuttled slowly to and fro through the slow rain, as the few ambulances brought more and more men from nearer the front. As the day began to wane, Carnegie, who had exchanged a few words with Charlie and sent a few messages through him, noting the boy's pale, worn face as he did so, said

32

to him, "Come on, son, go into town with us. This will be our last trip."

"The office told me last night," said Charlie, "that if I left my post without permission, I'll be shot."

"But surely they didn't expect you to stay here forever," exclaimed Mr. Carnegie. "Nonsense! How long have you been here on continuous duty?"

"Four days."

"Had anything to eat today?"

"Four or five crackers and some salt pork—and some berries from out there alongside the railroad track."

"Well, I'm from the War Department, and I order you to come back to Washington at once."

"But if I'm needed here—" Charlie was not resisting too hard.

"Get on the train," ordered Carnegie with genial brusqueness. "That is an order."

It was obeyed. Next morning, when Charlie visited the War Office, he was told that in recognition of his faithfulness to duty, he had been granted a week's leave to visit his home in Ohio. Deducting travel time, he would have four days all told, at home. But as if that boon were not incredible enough, he was handed a hundred dollars in gold "for expense money"—five glittering double eagles—$20 gold pieces! He heard of no other operator being so rewarded, and subsequent experience convinced him that the War Department would never have been guilty of such generous weakness. Slowly it dawned upon him that his benefactor could have been nobody else but genial young Mr. Carnegie— though he never had this confirmed.

The Battle of Bull Run convinced the Government that the war was going to last much longer than had been expected; so Thomas Scott and Andrew Carnegie went back to their posts with the Pennsylvania Railroad, where they could be as useful to the nation as at Washington. It was perhaps well that Carnegie was withdrawn from touch with the War Department telegraph. Otherwise, he would have seen thereafter so many memorable instances of devotion to duty on the part of boy operators that he could not have rewarded them all as he did (or did he?) Charlie Jacques.

III

Bottled-Up Railroad

Until his startling introduction to old John Brown, Marion Kerner hadn't paid a great deal of attention to politics. He had heard and read much talk about "free soil" and "states' rights" and "bleeding Kansas," but he sketched through these topics lightly in the newspapers, thinking of them as questions that would eventually subside or be settled by compromises. But now he found that a crisis was approaching, something that could not be treated lightly. Debates in Congress, sometimes between men who carried concealed pistols, swelled to a bitter uproar. Threats of secession, a new word to Marion, were heard. In the hill country which lay back of Martinsburg, there were few people who owned slaves, and the prevailing sentiment there was against the South. "We ought to secede from Virginia," said some. "We ought to be a separate State."

Men said that never in the nation's history had there been so important, so fateful an election as that of 1860 would be. Southerners said it would probably be the last under the United States Government. If Marion had been old enough, he believed he would have voted for the Illinois rail-splitter. His Pennsylvania German forebears were all opposed to slavery and loyal to the national government. He became more tight-lipped as he heard men around him talking loudly on one side or the other.

"Keep your mouth shut," advised Mr. Bridges, the agent. "Don't have opinions, or if you do, don't mention 'em. This railroad is a lifeline, and we've got to keep it running. You're a railroad man, not a politician." So Marion bent his head lower over his table and said little when partisans squabbled in the waiting room, on the platform, even in his own office; for the rail employes were naturally divided in sentiment, and not many were as discreet as the young telegrapher.

The election of Lincoln in the fall of 1860 set a match to the fuse; States began seceding from the Union. With the firing on Fort Sumter in April, 1861, the war was on. Virginia sent troops to take possession of the United States armory at Harper's Ferry, with its stock of guns and ammunition. The divided loyalty of the rail employees was illustrated when a Virginia contingent of troops, traveling by train towards the Ferry, found its train stalled in climbing the grade up to Manassas Gap in the Blue Ridge. The engineer said he couldn't make his locomotive steam properly. The Confederate troop commander found that the engine crew had let their fire burn low. He drew a big navy pistol and ordered more wood in the furnace, and from there on, with him and his pistol in the cab, and plenty of wood in the fire-box, they made good time. The railroad had no end of trouble like this.

As these troops approached Harper's Ferry, a great light illumined the sky; the forty-five men in charge of the Armory had set fire to it and fled, destroying, among other things, 20,000 rifles and pistols.

The commander of the incoming Southern troops was a quiet, awkward-looking, black-bearded man from Lexington, a professor in the Virginia Military Institute named Thomas Jonathan Jackson. Three months were to pass before he received his deathless nickname of "Stonewall" on the battlefield of Bull Run. He had an increasing number of men under him, with headquarters at the Ferry and detachments scattered along the railroad in both directions. He had been there only two or three weeks when he executed a startling bit of strategy.

The railroad was double-tracked for 31 miles, from Martinsburg through Harper's Ferry to Point of Rocks, and the Federal Government was rushing coal as rapidly as possible from the West Virginia mines towards the Eastern seaboard for use in factories and warships. So Col. Jackson took pen in hand and wrote to John W. Garrett, President of the B. & O. Railroad in Baltimore, saying that the clatter of the night trains eastbound greatly disturbed the repose of his soldiers at Harper's Ferry and thereabouts, confined as they were closely to the tracks by the adjacent hills, and would he please arrange to have all his eastbound trains pass through Harper's Ferry between 11 A.M. and 1 P.M. daily, which would be feasible because of the long stretch of double track.

What Mr. Garrett said upon receiving this extraordinary request is not written in the history books, but realizing that the Confederate officer had the whip hand, he simmered down and wrote a polite reply, saying that the schedule would be rearranged according to Col. Jackson's wishes. Doing this was no small chore, and the B. & O. staff, from superintendents and dispatchers on down, used more bad language in the process than we even dare hint at. Marion didn't greatly care, for it reduced his labors considerably, and gave him more time for reading; but Bill, the day operator, was highly vocal on the subject.

Matters rocked along for a few days, and then here came another letter from Col. Jackson to Mr. Garrett. He pointed out that the westbound trains, especially long strings of empty coal cars, were still thundering over the switch frogs during the night, breaking the rest of his soldiers, and asked that they, as well as the eastbound trains, be bunched in those two hours around noon—that is, between 11 and 1 o'clock. With that long stretch of double track, this would be a simple matter.

"Simple, says he!" roared Mr. Garrett. His opinions of Col. Jackson as he strode about his spacious office, uttering wild and incoherent words and kicking his beautiful carved mahogany furniture with his fine custom-made boots, would better be passed over. He suspected something sinister about the whole affair, but even if he had guessed what it was, there was nothing he could do about it. "He's got us," he said at last to his assistant, slumping resignedly in his chair. "He has the guns and we haven't." Whereupon he wrote a letter of acquiescence to Col. Jackson, as suave as he could make it, though careful scansion would reveal that it was about to burst at the seams in two or three places and emit hot lava. He suggested that it would not be worth while running so many passenger trains during that two hours, so some of them might be discontinued. But with this, Col. Jackson—by wire—disagreed. There would be soldiers—officers and men—passing to and fro constantly, he said, and there should be passenger trains for them to ride on. So those trains were sandwiched in amongst the others, though at reduced speed.

Again there was the profane turmoil of rearranging the schedule. "Schedule!" growled a dispatcher. "There ain't any such

36

thing. The trains just creep along like a string of elephants holdin' to each other's tails." Bill, at Martinsburg, was fit to be tied. As it was evident that Marion would have little or nothing to do at night, he was ordered to share with Bill the duties of those two hours in nudging that mob of trains through the 31-mile stretch of double track.

For two days that was perhaps the hottest length of railroad in America. "If it keeps on, they'll melt the rails at this rate," said Bridges. On the third day, about 11:30 A.M., Bill had dodged out somewhere for a few minutes, as he found it convenient to do frequently when Marion was on the job with him. Marion noticed that a westbound freight train which had stopped just east of the station was swarming with soldiers in the bright uniform of the Virginia militia, which was the common garb of the Southern soldiers thereabouts before the Confederate government adopted the standard gray. There had been soldiers encamped all around the place since Jackson took over Harper's Ferry, but they had never interfered with trains or the railroad men at their work. Now he wondered why there were three or four of them on the engine and tender of the train. Another freight train, eastbound, came in sight west of the depot.

Just then a call came from Harper's Ferry. Marion's face was startled as he heard the unfamiliar finger on the key. Nearly every operator had his own personal touch, which was as well known—often more so—to other operators along the line as would have been his voice or his penmanship. This Harper's Ferry message was by an unknown hand. It said, brusquely, "Eastbound trains not coming fast enough. Rush them."

A strange message! "That's not Harper's Ferry," exclaimed Marion to someone who was entering the office at that moment, either Bill or Mr. Bridges, he supposed, and sitting down in the other chair. "I know Hec's fist as well as I know my own mother's handwrite, and that ain't—"

He was turning towards the newcomer as he spoke, and his eyes popped until they were like agate marbles as he discovered that the man was neither Bill nor Bridges, but a bearded Confederate officer, a lieutenant.

"Maybe there's a substitute at the Ferry," said the officer; "Hec may be sick or something." He smiled sarcastically.

"Yeh, maybe so," muttered Marion. Then looking out at the

37

eastbound train, slowing up just west of the station, he was struck by a thought. This officer probably couldn't read Morse . . .

"Gotta get orders for that train," he said, stabbing a finger at it. He began frantically calling Cumberland. He got a response and started to say—just as he heard another man entering the office behind him, "Rebel sold—"

A long arm reached over his shoulder and snatched his hand away from the key. He turned to face his assailant and saw that he was another stranger, a man in civilian dress.

"This young devil," said the latest comer to the officer, "was starting to report to somebody that Rebel troops had taken possession here. Better get him out of here, lieutenant."

"Come away from that table, boy," ordered the lieutenant. "You see, we have some telegraphers of our own. So you're a damn Yankee, are you?"

"I'm just an employee of the B. & O. Railroad," said Marion. "I'm not taking sides."

"You called us rebels," accused the lieutenant.

"That's what a lot of these people around here call you," defended Marion.

"Still, your taking up the word reveals your sentiments. Stand aside, there. Now, here comes the conductor of that train for his orders, I suppose. Write something for him, Morris," to the new operator, who had seated himself at the table. "Tell him," with a grin, "just to keep ambling on until somebody stops him."

The freight conductor came in almost simultaneously with Mr. Bridges and Bill. All stared wildly at the scene in the private office.

"Which is the conductor of that train?" asked the lieutenant. "You? Give him his orders, Morris."

"What's the number of your train?" asked Morris.

"No. 22," replied the amazed conductor.

The man wrote on a blank, "Conductor and engineer of train 22. Proceed cautiously eastward until stopped by flag."

"That ain't a legitimate order," protested the conductor.

"It's all you'll get," snapped the officer. "Look out there. See those soldiers on your engine? They're all armed, and your engineer will do just what they tell him to do. Go out and give him that order, and it won't make any difference whether you stay on the train or not. You won't be needed any more."

38

As the conductor went out in a sort of daze, Mr. Bridges spoke for the first time. "May I ask what's going on? I am the agent here."

"Glad to meet you," said the officer. He and Bridges mentioned their names and shook hands, though the lieutenant did not rise. "The fact is, we've sort of taken over here, Mr. Bridges," he added.

"So I see," agreed Bridges. "But you still haven't told me why."

"I'll explain a little later; haven't time now. You might as well take it easy in the waiting room. I don't know the schedule, but I don't think there'll be any more trains through here today, unless another one comes in from the west—we'll let that through, ha! ha! No, sit down in the waiting room and take it easy, Mr. Bridges, unless you have somewhere else to go. There won't be any tickets sold here today, ha! ha! Now, about these telegraphers; is this," indicating Bill, "the other one?"

"Yes," said Bridges, who had continued standing in the door.

"Why, I d-dunno," stammered Bill. "Yes, I guess so, if you'll pay me the same as the railroad—"

"Oh, the railroad and the commercial company will continue to pay your salary. The army of the Confederate States of America is merely here in a supervisory capacity." The lieutenant, in rare good humor, laughed again. "I just want to know if you will send the sort of telegrams we want sent."

"I—I guess I'll hafta do what I'm told," mumbled Bill, doggedly.

"All right, we'll keep you on, unless we catch you in any crooked business. Then it'll be prison for you. This other young spriggins, I wouldn't trust any further than I could throw a bull by the tail. Are you willing to work with us?" he demanded of Marion.

"I wish you'd let me go to my home in Pennsylvania," said Marion.

"Aha, so you are a damned Yankee! I was sure of it. No, we can't turn you loose just now. I know you key-pounders. You'd sneak in somewhere and tattle something by wire behind our backs. I think we'll have to lock you up for a while. Sergeant," to a petty officer, who had come over with a private from the westbound train, "know of any little doghouse where we can lock a man up for a few hours? We'll send him to Headquarters later."

The sergeant pondered. "I noticed a little tool-house jist acrost the tracks," he replied, pointing. "I guess I could git the key from the inspector."

39

"All right, put him there."

The eastbound train was rumbling by the station. As it passed, one saw soldiers on the engine, and soldiers in the caboose. Peering out from the caboose with round eyes was the little conductor, puzzled and frightened.

"Come along," said the sergeant, pulling Marion by the arm, and they crossed the tracks. The old greaser, Eb Boffin, was just putting away in the little shed his oil can, waste and hammer, preliminary to going to his noon dinner. He gave up his key perforce, and looked at Marion with sympathetic eyes.

"What're they lockin' ye up for, son?" he asked.

"General cussedness," replied the sergeant, humorously. He shoved Marion into the tiny, windowless hut, lighted only through crevices, cluttered with tools, grease and oil containers, and with no place to sit down but on the floor.

"I'll bring yuh a coupla crackers later," said he as he moved off, "if they's any left. I'll have to keep yer key, old man," to Boffin. "You won't be doin' any more work today, nohow."

Late that afternoon the lieutenant, gleeful with triumph, explained the situation to Bridges.

"The Confederacy needs more equipment for its railroads; cars —all kinds of cars—and locomotives. So Colonel Jackson arranged to trap most of your rolling stock between here and Point of Rocks, and at a given time, switch it all into the two railroads going up the Shenandoah Valley. He brought three telegraphers from stations up the Valley to take post here and at Harper's Ferry and Point of Rocks—the three most important spots, d'ye see. Soldiers were sent to the intermediate stations and to two stations beyond this and beyond Point of Rocks to stop all telegraphy this morning. Now, as rapidly as possible, all your trains are being siphoned into the Valley railroads at the Ferry and Shenandoah Junction. Pretty neat idea, don't you think?"*

"Very neat," admitted Bridges, sarcastically. "But how do you and Colonel Jackson think the railroad is going to do business, with most of its rolling stock stolen?"

The lieutenant spread his hands, with a look of surprised innocence. "That is the railroad's problem; outside our province. We did what we had to do, Mr. Bridges. This is war, you know."

*This fantastic episode was briefly described by the Confederate General John D. Imboden in *Battles and Leaders of the Civil War*, Vol. I, pp. 122-123.

"More like an insurrection, I call it," said Mr. Bridges.

"Take care we don't put you with your young telegrapher in the toolhouse," warned the officer.

This was not the only blow under which the B. & O. was reeling at the time. Several of its bridges—wooden, of course—were being burned in the West Virginia mountains. For a long time President Garrett fought sturdily to get his road back in running order again—borrowing cars and locomotives wherever he could, buying second-hand ones, ordering new ones built, patching up old rattletraps which had been standing on sidings for months and years because there were then no electric torches and no nervous haste to cut them into scrap as soon as they became a bit passe.

Marion passed the afternoon pretty uncomfortably. He stood for a while and leaned against the wall a while. Aside from the greasy floor, there was nothing to sit on but a jack, which he occupied for brief periods with a wad of cotton waste atop it, for a cushion; but there wasn't enough of the waste to make it comfortable. A soldier unlocked the door and proffered three hard crackers, which had to do for a midday meal. He heard that westbound freight train back eastward out of town, and not having the key to the situation, he was vastly puzzled, trying to figure out what was going on.

Peering through crevices as dusk approached, he was sure that they had no sentry guarding him. In fact, he couldn't see any soldiers anywhere. He had found a pinch-bar in a corner, and as it became darker, he began cautiously prying at the hasp of the door with it, trying not to make too much noise. The clatter of a passing wagon gave him his opportunity; with one mighty wrench he pulled the staple out of the aging wood, and was free.

His first look around him showed only a feeble oil street-lamp or two, lights in the depot and two or three stores, and few persons on the streets. Pulling his hat down over his eyes, he hurried to his boss's house, on the north side of town. Mr. Bridges and his wife welcomed him heartily, and pulling down the dining room shades, spread a bountiful supper for him.

"I was aiming to come down there with a couple of tools pretty soon and get you out of that shack," said Mr. Bridges. While Marion ate, he enlightened him on the events of the day.

41

"No, don't go to Pennsylvania," he urged, when Marion mentioned his plans. "Those fellows will be clearing out of here pretty soon, now that they've stolen our rolling stock, and you can get back on the job again."

"Suppose they try to catch me?"

"Frankly," said Mr. Bridges, "I think they'll be relieved to find that you've got away."

Somewhat deflated, Marion argued, "But if they've got all our engines and cars, how can the railroad operate?"

"I don't figure they got everything. I imagine we've got some odds and ends left, and Garrett can borrow or buy more. The B. & O. ain't out of business, you can lay money on that."

"I still think I'll head back to Pennsylvania. Maybe I can get a job there or enlist in the army."

Finding him obdurate, Mrs. Bridges made up a big package of food for him, and they lent him a blanket for a possible night bivouac. Mr. Bridges gave him traveling directions, and he trudged northward until he thought he must have gone three miles, when, finding a bit of turf against the wall of a shed abutting on the highway, he rolled himself in his blanket and slept until daybreak. He awoke in a dull, muggy dawn, ate some of his lunch, got a lift on a farm wagon across the Potomac to Williamsport, Maryland and walked thence through a slow rain to Hagerstown, where he arrived just before noon. He found a forest of tents and blue-coated soldiers just outside of town, and in one wall tent, rather larger than the others, a sound which halted him in his tracks; the click of a telegraph instrument.

Soaking wet, chilly and tired as he was, the sound was irresistible. Without hesitation, he lifted a flap and stepped inside the tent. Three young men, variously occupied—one was at a table, pounding a key—looked up in surprise at the bedraggled stranger.

"I heard the telegraph, and I couldn't pass it by," he explained. "I'm an operator myself." Then all at once, it seemed so dry and homey there with the rain pattering on the canvas, the clicking of the key so friendly and familiar that he forgot all about Pennsylvania. "I wonder if I could get a job," he blurted out.

"Have to ask Captain Gilmore," said one of the men, nodding at another who wore a golden-brown beard, though Marion, looking at him, thought the face above the beard was little, if any, older than his own.

Marion introduced himself, and sitting on a camp-stool, told the story of Jackson's coup, whilst the other three suspended their work and listened in breathless fascination, broken now and then by exclamations of astonishment.

"We'd just heard a hint of something looney going on down there," said Gilmore at the end of the story, "but nobody could give us the straight of it. If that ain't the slickest trick I ever heard of, then I'll be eternally ding-danged."

The three seemed lost in admiration at the enemy stroke.

"That piece of double-track with Harper's Ferry in the middle of it was made a-purpose for such a job," said one.

"Like a pocket for a pool ball," agreed Gilmore.

An orderly came in at this moment with a scribbled message. Gilmore glanced at it and handed it to Marion.

"Let's hear you send this to Secretary Cameron," said he.

Marion sat down at the table, a little nervous and began. He had not sent three words when the others looked at each other and nodded. He was an op, all right, and a good one.

"You'll do," said Gilmore at the end of the message. "Where were you headed when you came here? Pennsylvania? Why Pennsylvania? Nothing happening in Pennsylvania. The army can use good men like you. We'll drive that rebel gang off the B. & O. in a few days, and you can go back to Martinsburg, if you like, or better still, in the field; lots more fun. They're sending ops out with army commanders now, you know. I'll put you on rations, and you can help us here for a few days until I can get a regular job for you. Whaddya say?"

"Sounds fine, Captain," said Marion.

"And you can omit the 'Captain.' My name's Jim Gilmore. We haven't any rank in the telegraph service—not yet, anyhow. I just happen to be in charge of the local headquarters here, and civilians think I must have a title of some sort, so Captain it is. But it's bunkum; strictly for outsiders."

As predicted, the Federals soon took over the B. & O. again, Jackson retiring up the Shenandoah Valley, where he kept Union forces in continual hot water. Marion Kerner was sent to the western Virginia mountains where, under various commanders, most prominent of whom was General George B. McClellan, a lively little war was carried on in 1861 and '62 for the possession of the mountain area. A convention organized it in '61 as a separate Northern State under the name of Kanawha, unfortunately changed later to West Virginia, and it had a few Federal regiments of its own. After General McClellan left the area early in '62, West Virginia practically dropped out of the news and out of war history. Its partisans, however, North and South, slam-banged to and fro through mountain gaps and gorges, belaboring each each other fiercely though on a small scale which the outer world thought too insignificant to notice.

IV

Nancy Hart's New Dress

Over in West Virginia, Marion Kerner began to hear of a young woman scout and spy named Nancy Hart, who, contrary to the convictions of most mountain folk, was a violent Southern partisan. Plain, even homely and taciturn, she travelled unnoticed down into the Shenandoah Valley, scouting for General Jackson in his early days in that theater. Then she retired into the wilder parts of the mountains, her own home country, where she knew every rock and brook, and where she flitted about, ghost-like, the most daring of spies. The Federal Government offered a reward of $500 for her capture, and she became more elusive than ever.

Marion was stationed at Summersville, a tiny mountain county seat when, one late May day, a stir and babble of voices outside his tent attracted his attention, and looking out, he saw a group of soldiers apparently hustling a woman towards the courthouse.

"We caught that Nancy Hart," said a detached soldier to him, gleefully.

She had put up a sturdy fight against her captors. Her cotton dress was torn in several places, revealing dirty underwear and dirty bare skin. She was in her twenties, but most unattractive—coarse shoes, no hat and her hair wildly unkempt. Anyone near her became painfully aware of her need for a bath. Her face was grim, streaked with sweat, and her eyes glowed like a cat's with fury.

"Put her in the jail," said Colonel Starr of the Ninth West Virginia. "Not safe to have her anywhere else."

He lost no time in sending his claim to Washington for the $500 reward. Meanwhile, some of his men were grumbling amongst themselves that they should have the major part of the swag, as the Colonel had done little towards tracking down the woman

45

and had no part in bodily taking her prisoner. They were the ones who got clawed and bitten, and they couldn't see where the Colonel came in for more than $50, at the most.

Marion's interest and sympathy were aroused by the plight of this wild creature of the crag and forest, who now lay in a smelly little jail cell, under the shadow of death as a spy—though Colonel Starr showed no hurry in convening a court martial on her case. He was not keen on being the agency to put a woman to death.

A telegrapher, not being an enlisted man, had special privileges in the matter of talking to a commander. Marion sought out Colonel Starr and said, "Colonel, what if I got some material for that Hart woman to make a dress for herself."

"I don't see that she deserves any privileges," was the Colonel's opinion.

"But Colonel, her clothes are in shreds—not decent; not fit to appear in public."

"She won't be appearing in public much more, anyhow," retorted the Colonel, with a rough laugh.

"But even at the court-martial—and when you hang her or shoot her—to have her appear in filthy tatters would cause a scandal in the North, sir. President Lincoln wouldn't like it."

"See here, Kerner," snapped the Colonel, "I don't propose to be taught my business by a young snip of a telegrapher. You 'tend to your key-pounding and I'll handle military affairs."

"Very well, Colonel," said Marion, and turned away.

"But I don't mind," the Colonel amended himself, "if you want to get her a dress, though I don't see how she can make it up in that dark cell; and we certainly can't let her outside to do it."

To approach the ferocious woman on the subject required courage, but Marion believed that even a mountain woman must suffer agony of soul from being in the tattered, bedraggled condition in which she now found herself, and would listen to a suggestion for improvement. He explained his intention to the soldiers guarding the courthouse, but at first found little sympathy for the idea. If she wanted a new dress, was the general reaction, let her rebel friends provide it for her. But Marion, undiscouraged, approached the little window in the door of her cell and said, "Miss Hart."

At first, he had no reply. Peering through the opening, he with difficulty discerned her figure, sitting against the rear wall,

46

glaring at him with a malevolence that would have been poisonous if she could have made it so. For her, who had never in her life been shut up anywhere against her will, this imprisonment in a bad-smelling cell was well-nigh unbearable. Every hour, every minute of it added the bitterness of gall to her concentrated hatred.

Again Marion spoke, "Miss Hart."

"Yuh needn't try to soft-sawder me, young feller," snapped a voice from the cell—feminine, but with a razor-edge on it. "I got no time for philanderin'."

Marion had to smile at that. "I just happened to think," he said, "that as you got your dress torn some, maybe you wouldn't mind having a new one."

"I got no money to buy new clo'es," she muttered.

"But if some of us got some money together and bought the material—after all, it's our fault that your dress is torn. Can you sew?"

"I made the clo'es I got on. Any woman that's wuth her salt kin sew."

"Well, if I can find the material in the store here—and a needle and thread—"

"How'm I gointa cut the cloth?" she demanded, sarcastically.

"O, yes. scissors. Maybe I can borrow a pair of scissors."

"Don't let her have no scissors," warned the guard in a low tone. "She'll be stobbin' some of us with 'em, shore as the world."

"I don't see how you expect me to make a dress," she demurred, "shet up in this dark hole."

"I'll see that you're supplied with candles. But first, I guess you haven't had a chance to comb your hair for several days. Here's a comb for you—new, right out of the store."

For a few moments she did not move. Then she slowly walked to the window and took the comb from his hand, but did not utter a word of thanks. That she accepted it, however, was encouraging.

He managed to rustle a few nickels, dimes and quarters among the soldiers, went to the best of the two general stores and found some rather sombre gingham which was the only stuff available, though it was very expensive. Mrs. Paskins, the merchant's wife, gave advice on the quantity of material required for a "dress pattern," as it was called, and Marion found that the bill was more than he had expected.

"Well, I don't know," he said, fingering the coins in his pocket, "we hadn't looked for it to be so much . . . "

"The war has run everything up so high," explained the storekeeper. "Them Yankee cotton mills are takin' advantage—" he checked himself, flustered. His sympathies were Southern, but he naturally didn't want to let Union troops know it. But it moved him to help in the present situation.

"Tell you what I'll do," he said after getting a hint of the financial situation. "I'll throw off the difference—about a dollar, ain't it?—between the price of the goods and what you boys got. I can't say no fairer than that, can I?" He had thread but no needles in stock, and neither did the other store; but Mrs. Paskins lent a couple, running them through a bent piece of cardboard for carriage, and hoping they wouldn't be lost or broken. She also lent a pair of scissors, specifying that they must be returned to her, no matter what happened to the regiment or the Northern or Southern governments.

When the sentry-jailer opened Nancy's cell door, permitting Marion to enter with his package, she sat in stony silence as he laid it on her cot beside her.

"And here are some candles," he added, "and here," he presented a little paper packet, "are some matches. Be careful of them, for they're scarce."

She made neither move nor sound as he retired from the room.

"She ain't very polite, you gotta admit that," said the sentry, who had contributed a dime towards the project. But that she took a keen interest in it was proved by the prompt lighting of one of her candles to examine the cloth. A village woman, a Mrs. Exum, had been engaged to service the cell daily and carry her meals in to her, a sentry standing by with a gun trained on her to prevent slip-ups. This woman had already provided Nancy with some safety pins—only six; "It's all I had"—to pin her tattered raiment together, and she now undertook the task of helping her to fit her dress. What looked like a dirty white article of underwear was draped over the little window in the cell door; the opposite window of the cell, which opened on the outer air, was too high above the sloping ground to permit peeping.

They were the better part of five days on the job, including an

48

hour spent in searching for one of the needles one day when it was lost on the cell floor. Mrs. Exum's influence was seen in the design of the dress. Ladies were then wearing gowns with low necks, sometimes seemingly almost about to slip off the shoulders, and Mrs. Exum persuaded Nancy to follow the fashion to a limited extent. "You got fine shoulders," she complimented, "and it'd be a shame not to be in style." Nancy wouldn't go as far as her adviser desired, but she did make concessions. Finally, Mrs. Exum repaired and laundered the prisoner's undewear, and at Marion's suggestion, aided in preparing two tubs of water, one for soaping, the other for rinsing, so that she might have a bath.

"She says," Mrs. Exum reported to Marion, "the last time she had a washin' was in a branch nigh her home a month ago."

"Where does she live?"

Mrs. Exum shook her head. "That she won't tell."

"Is she married?"

Amusement glinted in Mrs. Exum's eyes. "She ain't tellin' that, either."

"Oh, I'm not thinking of proposing to her," Marion hastened to say. "I've just been wondering what her husband, if she has one, thinks of all this gallivanting around."

"From what I've seen of her," was Mrs. Exum's opinion, "he kin like it or he kin lump it."

Two or three days later a wandering photographer drifted into town and began to do a considerable business with the soldiers, making daguerreotypes of them for the pleasure of their folks at home.

"I want a picture of Nancy Hart," said Marion. With Colonel Starr's permission, he had her brought forth and explained the process to her, while three soldiers stood with guns at the alert. She had never seen a camera before, and was afraid of it.

"I ain't gonna have that thar thing take aim at me," she protested.

"But listen," argued Marion, "Several of the soldiers have been photographed. I'll tell you what I'll do. I'll let him photograph me right now, while you look on."

So he posed while Nancy watched intently, and the soldiers joked, "Look purty, Kerner," and "Smile for the gentleman."

"You see, that didn't do me any harm," he said. "Now let's see you pose for him."

She had become a bit more human since she'd had a bath and a new dress. Now she even smiled faintly as they made arrangements.

"She oughta have a hat on," said one of the soldiers.

"And put this feather in it," added another, producing a small plume such as many militia orgainziations wore when they entered the National army, and affixing it in the soldier's hat which they clapped on her head.*

This amiable episode and Nancy's seemingly mellower mood made her guardians careless. On the third day later, Marion was working at his key in his tent when he heard the crash of a musket shot, a confusion of yells, the galloping of a horse and more gunshots. He ran out and was confronted by an astounding fact.

When Mrs. Exum entered her cell that morning, Nancy had with elaborate casualness, moved to the door. Reconnoitering through the door-window, she saw a horse standing a few yards away with bridle lying loosely on its neck—Colonel Starr's mount, which would stand quietly wherever its rider left it. The Colonel was standing in the door of the courthouse, several yards away, talking to a citizen. Nancy's jailer, a gangling, slow-witted hillman, was standing with a gun held loosely in his hands, his head turned to gawk at a group of three or four other soldiers, who, with guns leaned against the fence, were gossiping on the other side of the street.

With the quickness of a cat, Nancy Hart hurled the door open, seized the unlucky guard's gun, with the same motion jammed the muzzle against his body, and without putting the stock to her shoulder, pulled the trigger. With a strangled cry, the man fell dead, shot diagonally through heart and lung. The killer, her eyes glittering with the fury of a tigress, leaped over his body and ran the thirty feet to Colonel Starr's horse. Mountain women have never worn long skirts. The rough terrain in which they live, the morning dew- and rain-wet weeds and bushes make shorter skirts desirable. So she was little impeded by her clothing, and unsoftened by eleven days of imprisonment. With one leap she bestrode the horse, and with a yell, a slap of her hand and a kick of her heels on its sides, she sent it galloping, she lying flat

*Miraculously enough, that little tintype survived for more than half a century. You may see a reproduction of it in the *Photographic History of the Civil War*, vol. 8.

over its withers. The idling soldiers stared for a moment, then snatched up their guns and began firing.

"Don't shoot the horse! Don't shoot the horse!" cried Colonel Starr, dancing in frenzied excitement. This practically insured the escape of the spy, for she lay so flat on her steed that she presented a poor target.

"Chase her!" howled the discomfited Colonel, as he saw his $500 reward go glimmering, along with his highly prized horse. "Why didn't I have her shot long ago?" he wailed. But now there was no horse ready saddled. Nancy knew her country, and by the time pursuit was really begun, she was far in the lead. She threaded footpaths and made short cuts where the horse had to scramble terrifically and sometimes fell—Colonel Starr would have wept to see it—but which soon had her pursuers baffled. Colonel Starr's state of mind is beyond being described.

Marion Kerner was soon moved to a more important post, and he was therefore not present on that morning at the crack of dawn when something like a tornado burst upon the camp of the two companies of the 9th West Virginia as Summersville. The surprise was devastating. Colonel Starr and his under-officers were routed out of bed in their shirt-tails, given only time to don breeches and shoes; most of the privates were also taken prisoner. All the horses were seized and most of the guns, leaving some forty men behind, with no mounts and few arms. The Colonel's humiliation and fury were almost unbearable when he saw, in the dawning light, Nancy Hart, sitting decorously side-saddled on his horse (he groaned as he saw its knees, skinned in her rough-and-tumble flight), silently watching, with a grim ghost of a smile, the progress of the raid which she had guided to its target.

Marion Kerner heard little more of her after that. In fact, it was not long until he himself was captured and sent first to Belle Isle and then to Libby Prison, where he remained a long time before he was finally exchanged and returned to service. His subsequent telegraph activities were not greatly eventful. But thirty years after the war, he wrote a song which was often sung at gatherings of the Old-Time Telegraphers' and Historical Association:

'TWAS A BOY THAT SWUNG THE KEY

When our country was in danger of destruction,
    And fathers, sons and brothers stood as foes,
When North and South were threatened with disruption
    And war clouds thickened fast as they arose;
A speedy call, "To arms!" aroused the Nation
    Whose loyal sons would save her unity;
When our President sent forth his proclamation,
    'Twas a boy, a loyal boy, that swung the key.

CHORUS: 'Twas a boy, a loyal boy, that swung the key
        That led a Nation safe to victory.
        Let his memory never perish,
        May a grateful country cherish
        The boy, the loyal boy that swung the key.

While statesmen gathered close in contemplation,
    Our soldiers in their tented camps prepared
To sacrifice their lives to save the Nation
    If foes its dissolution ever dared.
But when from Sumter came the declaration
    That war alone shall solve our destiny,
'Twas a thrilling news that flashed to all the Nation
    By a boy, a loyal boy who swung the key.

From Appomattox came a declaration,
    "Secession shall forever buried be."
The Union is cemented as a Nation
    The hand of Grant is nobly grasped by Lee.
Thank God, the struggle's over and Old Glory
    Waves proudly over land and o'er the sea.
'Twas a boy that gave the world the joyful story,
    'Twas a boy, a loyal boy who swung the key.

V

The Youngest Op

"John," said his older brother Richard, one spring day in 1858, "here's a telegram going to a man out in the country west of here; about five miles, I guess."

He didn't say, "Can you take it?" or "Will you take it?" John, aged nine, was the messenger boy for the office, and whoever served the telegraph in those days didn't refuse to tackle any job that confronted him.

Richard O'Brien was the third or fourth successor as operator at Greensburg, Pennsylvania, to Joe Taylor, for whom young Andy Carnegie had once substituted. He served both the Pennsylvania Railroad and the commercial telegraph line which passed through the town, At this time Richard was a mature person of 17, John eight years younger. In those days, people were becoming accustomed to seeing boys in their latter teens running telegraph offices. Two years before this, when he was only 15, Richard had been operator at Downingtown, nearly 300 miles farther westward; and there little John at seven, began delivering a few messages around the town. When Richard was transferred to Greensburg, John and their mother went with him.

"The nearest way to this man Trumpel's house," said Richard, tapping the telegram with his finger, "is along the railroad track for a coupla miles; then turn off to the right just beyond a bridge, and begin inquiring your way. Any of the farmers can tell you where he lives. But if you're going through the tunnel—"

"Of course I'm going through the tunnel," interrupted John. "I've been through it before. I ain't gointa climb over that hill."

"Well, be awfully careful about trains in there," Richard cautioned.

"There are places where I can stand out of reach of the train," said John. The tunnel, like many another in early days, had not been walled. A hole had just been blasted through the limestone of the hill, and when it was large enough, the rough stone sides were left as they were. As John had said, there were nooks in which one could stand, safe from the trains.

"Better go home and eat dinner right now," ordered Richard. "It'll take all afternoon for you to go out there and back. Let's see—the accomodation'll come along—or it should—before you reach the tunnel. You'll be past the tunnel before the local freight comes along—if it ever does. The Fast Line is what you'll have to watch out for; it will be along while you're on your way home. I'm worried about that train."

"Nobody that ain't asleep needs be hit by a train," boasted John. "No, I won't take a lantern; too heavy. It'd wear me out, carryin' it out there and back. I'll just take a new candle and some matches."

Richard stared at the table for a moment, calculating whether a full-length candle would last through the tunnel twice, and decided that it would. People were accustomed to taking risks in those days, especially if they were young. He went on—

"That man ought to pay you something—a dime, anyhow—for taking a message out there. He shouldn't expect us to deliver a telegram five miles in the country for nothing. But don't quarrel with him. And be sure to get home before dark. Don't stop to throw rocks at birds and squirrels. Mother'll be worried about you."

Mother *was* worried—about that tunnel—but "must" was a powerful word then, and like everybody else, she took a chance. John lighted his candle and trudged through the long bore, whistling to keep up his spirits. He found the way to Trumpel's farm without trouble, and delivered the telegram. Trumpel, a hard-faced man, signed for it and read it while John waited.

"Is there any answer?" asked John.

"No."

Still John waited. "Ain't you gointa pay anything for the delivery of the message?" he asked.

"It was prepaid by the man who sent it," retorted Trumpel, whacking it with his hand.

"It's addressed to you at Greensburg," John pointed out; "prepaid only to Greensburg—not five miles out in the country. We didn't have to bring it out here."

"Then what did you do it for?"

"I was ordered to do it," said John, "because the company wants to be kind and polite to everybody. Looks to me like you oughta be willing to pay as much as a dime to a messenger for walkin' ten miles."

"Oh, so you'd get it all, then."

"Well. I do all the walking," John reminded him.

"You don't get a cent from me," snapped Trumpel and turned to enter the house.

A hot retort sprang to the boy's lips, but he recalled Richard's warning, "Don't quarrel with him," so he said nothing, but turned and began his long trek towards town. Then and there he decided he was tired of being a messenger.

His anger evaporated as he walked homeward, being tempted to loiter by the sights and sounds of the forest which bordered most of the track. But as last he quickened his pace as he realized that the afternoon was rapidly slipping away. He was in the deep cut approaching the tunnel when he heard the roar of the "Fast Line" behind him and shrank into a niche in the rock. The engine crew must have both seen him; the fireman lifted a hand in greeting, and he wondered if the fireman knew who he was and would tell Richard he was on his way. Somehow, the smoke-filled tunnel seemed more eerie than before, and he whistled more loudly as he stepped from tie to tie, and heard the drip, drip, drip of water from the ceiling.

"Dick," were his first words upon reaching the station, "I want to learn to operate. I'm tired of being a messenger. That old skeezicks wouldn't give me a cent."

"Well, I will," said Richard, producing a dime. "And I'll teach you the alphabet, but you can't get a job right away. They would think you are—rather young."

"Oh, pshaw, I could handle an office as well as anybody," boasted John.

Richard looked at him quizzically. "It might surprise you to know," he said, "that some folks consider me pretty young for my job, and I'm eight years older than you are. But I'll teach you how to send."

John continued to deliver telegrams as he practiced the Morse alphabet on a temporarily idle key. At that time they still had receiving machines in the offices, which recorded the dots and dashes of incoming telegrams on a paper tape, and from this the receiving operator wrote out the message in script. But operators were coming more and more to make a habit of not waiting for the tape, but taking the message by ear and writing it out as the key clicked it off. "But don't you try to do this," warned Richard.

But Dick was outside, talking to a train conductor one day when the Greensburg call, "V"—represented by three dots and a dash—came. John clicked back, "I I", meaning I am ready to receive, started the register tape going, and when the message was completely sounded off, stopped the tape and copied out the dispatch. When Richard hurried in, he read the tape, then the copy, and nodded approvingly. After that, John frequently took messages by the register.

One day a trainman came hurrying, out of breath, along the track. "We're wrecked in Carr's Cut," he panted. "Lotta people hurt. Notify headquarters."

Richard called Altoona and reported the news. "Take an instrument and go to the wreck," he was ordered. "Cut in on the wire and tell us developments. We will send wrecking train."

"John, you'll have to take charge of the office here for a while," said Dick, hurriedly collecting an instrument and a few yards of wire. "Do the best you can, but above all, be careful; be accurate." He hurried away on a hand car.

It wasn't long before a call came and a message was spelled out for "J. C. Clarke & Q"—a least, so the address seemed to John. He knew Mr. Clarke, a business man in town, but he didn't know of any "Q" connected with him. He wrote out the telegram and took it to Mr. Clarke, two or three blocks away.

"—& Q?" said Mr. Clarke, looking puzzled.

"Yes, sir," said John. "Isn't the message all right?"

"Oh, yes, I understand the message, but what gets me is who this man Q is. I don't know him."

A thought struck John. He took the telegram from Mr. Clarke's hand, read it again and blushed.

"I guess I made a mistake," he admitted. "A dot, a space and three dots means '&', but E is one dot, s is three dots, and the space between 'em should be a little longer than if it was &. That's intended for Esq.—J. C. Clarke, Esq."

It was not uncommon in those days for senders of telegrams to add "Mr." or "Esq." to the name of the addressee.

Mr. Clarke laughed uproariously, and sometimes teased John thereafter when he saw him with "Ever locate that fellow Q yet, Johnny?"

Within a few months John was receiving messages by ear and sending like a real "op." He talked with other telegraphers along the line—some of them in their teens—and with division officials at Altoona. None of them knew how young he was.

"Those O'Briens just naturally take to the telegraph," said people in Greensburg to each other. "They must have telegraph wires for nerves."

"Now Dick," said John, "if you'll tell me what to say, I'll write to Mr. McCargo, and apply for a job as an extra."

Richard stared at him with a humorous quirk around his lips. "This beats anything I ever heard of," he said. "An infant ten and a half years old applying for a job as an operator. Are you going to let him know how young you are?"

"Of course not," said John, reddening. "What difference does that make if I can do the work?"

"It might make a lot of difference to some people," Richard commented. He still hesitated, but at last, after some debate, he said, "All right, I'll suggest a letter, but you must forget that I did it. Remember, this is strictly your own idea; you did it unbeknownst to me."

So John wrote a letter to David McCargo, superintendent of telegraphs for the Pennsylvania at Altoona, applying for a position as extra operator, to go anywhere at any time. He wrote in his best hand—somewhat schoolboyish, it is true, but after all, many men wrote and still do, that sort of script—copied it three times before he was satisfied with it, and then made another copy to send to Joseph Kerbey, a sub-chief at Pittsburgh. He felt on firmer ground here, for he had talked by wire with Kerbey more than once; Kerbey knew that he was Dick O'Brien's younger brother, and though he had never seen him, he knew that the unseen John O'Brien had a good fist at the key. It is an indication of the easy-going casualness with which business was done then that a wire

57

promptly came back from Kerbey, "Hold yourself in readiness for a call."

This threw John into a high state of delight. He began expecting the call by the next day. By the third day he was saying, "I wonder why that call don't come." But days and weeks passed and still no word came from Pittsburgh. Richard tried to explain to him that there were probably many others on the waiting list, which wasn't what he wanted to hear.

"John," said Richard one day, "Swengle, that new repair man on the O'Reilly line, needs a helper. Maybe you better go with him for a few days."

The O'Reilly was the commercial telegraph line, owned by the Eastern Telegraph Company, and roughly paralleling the railroad line from Philadelphia to Pittsburgh. Where it touched the railroad, operators for the railroad line also handled O'Reilly business. It was cheaply constructed, with sapling poles and the insulators were little earthenware troughs over which the single wire ran. Wind sometimes blew the wire out of the groove; wind and sleet caused the poles to lean, and at times the wire sagged until it touched the ground or bushes or fences, which made sending difficult, if not impossible.

"But my call may come from Mr. Kerbey while I'm away," objected John.

"Call me at every station," said Dick, "and I'll let you know if the word comes."

John, still reluctant, agreed to go, though grumbling. He found Swengle, the new repair man, a greenhorn, and not keen about work. John had to help him dig around leaning poles and prop them up; when there was repair trouble, he had to shin up the pole—for they had no climbers—and attend to it, and he had to help carry the tools. By the time they had done the ten-mile stretch to Latrobe, John was so dead tired that he couldn't stay awake to finish his supper at the little hotel, and next morning he couldn't remember going to bed. But when he awoke that morning, his mind was made up.

"Mr. Swengle," he announced, "I'm through! I'm going back to Greensburg. I'm so stiff and sore I can hardly walk. I'm an operator, not a lineman. You can pick up somebody around here to help you."

He didn't visit the telegraph office, little guessing how soon he

58

was to see Latrobe again. Dick was somewhat annoyed when he showed up at home again. "I was doing most of the work," John explained, (At least, it seemed so to him), "and one day just about wore me out. Hear anything from Pittsburgh?"

"No."

But the word came a few days later, and it was a hurry call. "Proceed to Latrobe on No. 2 to replace Operator Head for a week," chattered the ticker. "Do not miss train. Conductor Harris will have your pass, will be looking for U."

John found himself on air, but it did not dizzy him. Richard was out of the office at the time. No. 2 was due in ten minutes, and always stood at the station for at least five minutes, for those were leisurely days; and John had a telegram to deliver. It did not occur to him to leave it for Dick to handle. He himself was the messenger, and he must do his job. Leaving the office untended, he ran all the way to the office of the addressee of the telegram, found it locked, ran to two other places to find him, meanwhile hearing the train pull in—right on time, drat it! Nine out of ten other times, it would be late. Running back as hard as he could pelt, he saw the conductor raise his hand to the engineer and swing aboard as the train slowly got into motion. There was no time to notify his brother, no time even to look at the telegraph office. John grabbed a handle and scrambled aboard the moving steps on his knees, at the imminent peril of his life. He was breathless and still shaking like a leaf from strain and nervousness when the conductor entered the car.

"Mighty nigh missed the train," he gasped. "My name is John O'Brien. Mr. Kerbey said you would have my pass. I'm going to Latrobe."

The conductor stared in amazement and skepticism at the peach-cheeked passenger. "Mr. Kerbey said a man—" he began.

"I guess he said a telegrapher, didn't he?" ventured John, smiling, and turning pink, too. "I'm an operator. I'm going to Latrobe to take Dick Head's place for a week." He drew from his pocket the copy of Kerbey's telegram. The conductor was getting used to teen-age telegraphers, but this was the first time he had ever met a mere child claiming to be an operator. Still gazing at John, he took the message and read it.

"How old are you?" he asked.

"Nearly eleven."

The conductor handed the telegram back to him and went along the aisle, shaking his head.

John knew that something of the sort was due to happen at Latrobe. When he left the train, Dick Head, the agent, was outside, looking after baggage. John walked into the office and sat down. When he came in, it was his turn to stare.

"What can I do for you?" he asked.

"I'm John O'Brien," was the reply, "come to take your place while you're off." He handed over Kerbey's telegram. Head read it and sank into a chair, flabbergasted.

"You don't mean to say that Kerbey sent you to do the operating here, do you?" he asked.

"Yes, sir, I've talked to you by wire more than once," said John.

Just then the key began clicking "K", "K", "K", the call for Latrobe. Head rose to go to the table, but John said, "Hold on. I'll take it for you." He wrote out the message in his boyish but legible script and gave the paper to the agent. Head looked at it as if in a daze, but finally made a copy of it in his own hand, put this into an envelope and without a word, went out, supposedly to deliver it.

The addressee must have been near by, for Head was back in five minutes. "Now, John," said he, "I guess you're an operator all right, but don't try to tell me that you're a ticket agent and a freight agent, too."

"I never sold a ticket yet," admitted John, "but I reckon I could."

"Well, you handle the telegraph, and I think maybe I can get my brother to do the freight and tickets."

Just then a boy of twelve or thirteen and larger than John came in and tossed his telegraph messenger's receipt book down on a table. "Bert," said Head, "this is John O'Brien, who will take my place while I'm gone."

This time, it was Bert who was goggle-eyed, stricken speechless. The chief joy of John's stay at Latrobe was that of giving orders to Bert.

John's next relief job was at Willmore, and then McCargo sent him to Spruce Creek to replace one of three women operators on the line for a month. The office there was just a small box for reporting trains; there was no ticket agent. The village of Spruce

Creek was scarcely visible to the naked eye, and its situation, deep in the gorge of the brawling little Juaniata River, with steep mountain slopes towering all around, made it seem even lonelier.

One day a genial, kindly, bearded gentleman in his twenties, handsome but with only one eye—the other had been lost in an accident with a jar of acid when he was an operator—dropped off a train and announced himself as David McCargo, superintendent of telegraphs for the Pennsylvania Railroad. He visited pleasantly with the boy between trains, but just before his departure he said, gently, "John, I think it would make a better impression on people if you kept your stockings pulled up and your shoes neatly tied. Remember, you represent the Pennsylvania Railroad."

John turned beet-red, corrected those faults and was never guilty again.

After that, he substituted at Hollidaysburg, Duncannon and other places. He was on the staff of the superintendent's office at West Philadelphia in April, 1861, when Richard was ordered into military service. "Get me a job with the Army, too, Dick," he pleaded again and again, for the brothers corresponded regularly. Richard promised to do the best he could, but it was no easy chore. He was working for a different sort of employer now—crotchety, unpredictable, badly muddled Uncle Sam, a boss whose right hand, at the time, scarcely knew what his left hand was doing. For several months Richard was at the Pennsylvania depot in Washington, busy with wires regarding troop trains from the North. Then in the fall he and some other operators were shepherded by Jim Gilmore down to Fortress Monroe, at the mouth of the James River, destined to be a strong Federal base throughout the war; and from Headquarters in January, '62, came the order for John O'Brien to report there, too.

John resigned instantly from the Pennsylvania Railroad employ, collected as much of his salary as he could, and went back to his lodgings, walking on air. He was just three months past his thirteenth birthday. He took the railroad to Baltimore and a steamer from there down Chesapeake Bay to the fort. He had no difficulty in finding it; it was right by the water. Seeing an arched stone entrance, he headed for it, and amazingly enough, walked right in without being challenged by anybody; in fact, there was nobody at the entrance. He traversed a corridor which penetrated

61

the great wall of the fort, crossed a small parade ground, past some brass cannon and piles of cannonballs, and seeing a wire overhead, followed it into a large room, where some tables and desks were scattered about—one table having telegraph instruments on it—and some officers and non-coms, standing or sitting, talking or writing.

Richard was not visible anywhere. John headed for the telegraph table, sat down at it and ticked out "?", just to see what would happen. Immediately, someone answered, "Who is that?"

"John O'Brien," was the answer. "134" (Who are you?)

"George Cowlam, Newport News." Cowlam was an older operator. He must have been well up in his twenties!

"Do you know where my brother Richard is?" was John's next query.

"He can't be far away from you there. I was just going to call him. I have a message. Can you take it?"

There were some sheets headed, "United States Military Telegraph" on the table. John drew them towards him, and clicked, "GA" (Go ahead).

He received and wrote down the message. As he finished it, he looked up and saw that everybody in the room was watching him. Several of the officers had moved nearer to him, and a slender, white-haired man whose two stars on his shoulder-straps marked him as a general officer, was standing close beside him. John handed him the telegram, he read it, nodded and patted the boy on the head.

"My boy," said he, "you are very young to be able to do that."

John, who had promptly guessed the old man to be General John E. Wool, veteran of the War of 1812 and the Mexican War, and now commandant at Fortress Monroe, had risen to his feet. "I have been doing it at fifteen stations on the Pennsylvania Road for three years past, General," said he.

The next question was, "How old are you?" When he said "Thirteen, sir," the officers looked at each other in amazement and incredulity. But when General Wool heard that he had just arrived, that he walked right in through the open gate without being challenged, he blew up. "This is how our portal is kept!" he raged. "This boy might have been Jeff Davis or Beauregard; it would have been all the same. Wilson," to a lieutenant, "whoever is at the gate now, throw him in the guard-house and put somebody there who will stay there."

That sort of negligence never happened again; the portal was strictly guarded. John, however, had a pass which even permitted him to walk on the ramparts and the water-battery. He was always thrilled when a big sentry, with bayonet held aport, halted him and demanded the countersign—whereupon John would step nearer and whisper, "Seward" or "Chapultepec" or whatever it was that day.

Northerners, whether in the army or not, had plenty of opportunities to learn the song which had become almost a Confederate national hymn—"Dixie." John strode into the main room at the fort one day, whistling it *fortissimo,* and discovered a group of black-clad gentlemen in stovepipe hats sitting in conference. Then he saw his brother gesturing violently at him.

"John," exclaimed Richard in a shocked tone. "Haven't you any decency at all—dashing in here, whistling that rebel tune right in the presence of the President!"

He had tried to keep his voice low, but the men in the group heard it, or at least, one of them did—a tall, angular, loose-jointed man with a homely but good face, who smiled and waved a hand reassuringly. "Don't worry, son," he said. "It's all right. Dixie is one of my favorite tunes."

John subsided into a corner and watched him eagerly until he and the other men departed. It was his first and last glimpse of Abraham Lincoln.

At first, the Yankee troops held only the tips of the peninsula at Fortress Monroe and Newport News. Small forces of Confederates were so near that efforts to keep a telegraph line open between the two points were hampered by the Johnnies' playful way of cutting and carrying off half a mile or so of wire every now and then. Richard and John O'Brien, with a number of Negro workmen, were out along the line, restringing wire one day, when one of the Negroes exclaimed, "Looka yonder at dem Reb cavalry a-comin'!"

Everybody looked, and sure enough, there was a troop approaching at full gallop. The Negroes broke for the woods, and John tried to keep pace with them, but was soon left far behind. Richard, dodging behind a tree, studied the approaching horsemen and vainly yelled to his helpers to stop. The newcomers were Union cavalry.

Across the vast estuary of the James lay Norfolk, with an estuary of its own, the Elizabeth River, coming down to the James. Up that twisting inlet, invisible from Fort Monroe, was the Gosport Navy Yard, which had been taken over by the Confederates when the Union troops retired from Norfolk a few months before. There had been gossip circulated in some mysterious way of their own among Negro "contrabands"—escaped slaves taken under Federal protection—that the Rebs were building there in the Navy Yard a bomb-and-ball-proof floating monster ironclad, the like of which was never seen before. This was discounted on the Union side as the exaggerated yarns of ignorant men.

Some United States warships—all wooden, of course—had arrived in Hampton Roads, the great harbor at the mouth of the James, and caused the Confederates on the Peninsula to draw back a little. On March 8th, 1862, several of the best Union warships—*Congress, Cumberland, Minnesota, Roanoke*, and *St. Lawrence,* were lying scattered about the Roads at anchor, expecting no evil. John, on the ramparts of the fort, saw a small group of officers peering through field-glasses and a telescope at a column of black smoke arising from something moving out of the Elizabeth River estuary, and fully 15 miles away. The officers were discussing it excitedly as it drew nearer; "Never saw anything like it;" "Got no masts;" "Must be that monster the niggers've been talking about;" "Coming to fight our ships"—

John had heard enough. He rushed down to his instrument and called George Cowlam at Newport News. Richard, who was on the night trick at the time, was sleeping. "Got any field glasses?" was John's first question to Cowlam.

"There's a pair near by," replied George. "Why?"

"Look at that thing coming out of Norfolk. Must be that iron monster we've been hearing about—" Cowlam waited to hear no more, but bolted for the glasses. In a few minutes he could see it without glasses. It was indeed the "monster," the *Merrimac*, or *Virginia*, as the Confederates rechristened her, which they had rebuilt on the hull of a wooden ship, making the superstructure a massive box of very heavy timbers with sloping sides, heavily plated with iron, and with a sharp iron prow just under water,

Soldiers stringing wire on the battlefield, 1861.

Soldiers establishing wire communications.

Nancy Hart, Confederate spy. She wouldn't have smiled if they had asked her.

Army of the Potomac battery and operator wagon, late in the war.

which could ram into a wooden hull and open a gash that would soon sink it. It steered directly for the *Cumberland* and *Congress,* which were lying nearest to Newport News. They opened fire on it first, and saw their balls glance upward from its sloping sides, which had been greased! The *Merrimac* replied and the battle was on.

Cowlam had what might be called a ringside seat for the show. His set was too weak to reach Washington, and so at each move, he described it to John at the fort, who in turn repeated it to the War Department. It was like a hideous precursor of a modern sports broadcaster's blow-by-blow description of a boxing match; "She is steering straight for the *Cumberland"*—an anxious pause "The *Cumberland* gives her a broadside . . . she keels over . . . seems to be sinking . . . no, she comes on again . . . she has struck the *Cumberland* and poured a broadside into her . . . God! the *Cumberland* is sinking!" A long pause. "The *Cumberland* has fired her last broadside."

Next the *Merrimac* turned her attention to the *Congress,* and the solid shot and shell which by chance missed that ship began passing through Cowlam's shack; so he soon had to cease his chronicle and look to his personal safety. Having riddled the *Congress,* the *Merrimac* had only to deal with the *Minnesota,* which had run aground. But it was now late in the day, the tide was low and because of her great daught, the *Merrimac's* commander did not dare venture into uncertain waters, so he took his boat back to the Navy Yard.

That night the *Monitor,* the "Yankee Cheese Box on a Plank," arrived, and next day she fought the *Merrimac* to a standstill. The latter retreated to Norfolk Harbor, and came out again only once more, a few days later, when finding the *Monitor* still standing by the wooden ships, she retired again to the Navy Yard, this time to stay.

Some may be surprised to find an operator becoming exclamatory and profane by taps on a brass key, but the excitement was not uncommon among the boys, and the profanity occasionally burst from the keys of the older ones. An operator once went all the way from Memphis to Cincinnati to lick a man who had called him an offensive name by wire.

The thrilling episode of the two ironclads and the sinking of two ships of war before his eyes gave young John O'Brien a shocking glimpse into the realities of war. He was to have deeper insight before many weeks had passed. For now an army was swarming down Chesapeake Bay and landing near the end of the peninsula between the York and the James, with intent to capture the Confederate capital. "On to Richmond!" was the slogan at Washington and in the Northern newspapers. Some 400 vessels shuttled to and fro between the Peninsula and Northern ports, pouring out on the Virginia soil thousands of men, hundreds of horses, mules and covered wagons, artillery, ambulances, rations and munitions of war. Soon new blue uniforms, singing, skylarking, enjoying the great adventure—58,000 of them in all—spread great white tent cities for miles up the Peninsula. General McClellan, the Commander-in-chief, strode grandly ashore with his staff, resplendent in gold braid.

Parker Spring headed a corps of telegraph line builders, extending wires through the camps to the various generals' headquarters. It was unsafe to try to maintain a wire overland through Virginia to Washington, so a submarine cable, a section of the unsatisfactory Atlantic cable of 1858, was laid across Chesapeake Bay to the Eastern shore, up which a land wire ran through a territory which seemed safe from molestation, to Wilmington, and thence down to Washington.

On April 3rd a steamer arrived from Washington with eight more operators, including some destined to become noted—A. Harper Caldwell, Jesse H. Bunnell, John R. Emerick, Charlie Jacques, Brainard Lathrop, Henry Smith and Charlie Snyder. There were also some distinguished passengers aboard—the Comte de Paris and two or three other French noblemen who were volunteer aids on the staff of General McClellan. President Lincoln and Secretary Seward came down to Alexandria to see them off. Caldwell was General McClellan's own operator and cipher expert, and the other ops were distributed among the corps and division commanders.

And now the Army of the Potomac was ready to begin its drive toward Richmond. Yorktown, 25 miles away on the York River, was the first objective, but the small force of Confederates there escaped and went up the Peninsula to join General Johnston's army, only a few miles away. The Federals pursued and on May 5th caught up with the enemy at Williamsburg. All through that wet, gloomy day, the growling rumble of cannon could be heard as far away as Newport News. Then the greycoats retired towards Richmond, leaving 400 wounded in Union hands.

Now a sense of the horrors of war really burst upon the sensitive soul of thirteen-year-old John O'Brien. His cheek paled as he heard of scenes on the field hospitals; men with shattered legs and arms screaming with pain as the surgeons, without the slightest hint of anaesthetics, still unavailable, sawed and chopped off the useless remnants: and when, two days later, Jesse Bunnell and Charlie Jacques, at Headquarters, began sending the list of names of 1,500 dead and wounded in that fight, to be transmitted to Washington, John, choking with emotion, wrote them down with a tear occasionally slipping down his cheek. During the succeeding two months, as the shockingly greater casualty lists came in from Seven Pines and the Seven Days' Battles, and hospital camps full of mutilated men spread over the lower Peninsula, the boy's sensibilities became more inured to butchery, although it always set his nerves on end.

As the Army of the Potomac moved up the Peninsula, a new telegraphic technique was developed. The telegraph kept pace with the Army, even with the headquarters of division and corps commanders. Sapling poles, with an insulator at the top of each, were hastily planted by the linemen. Two men carrying a reel of wire on a palanquin between them, walked, or if under fire, dog-trotted along the line, with the wire unreeling and the linemen stringing it to the poles behind them. "Relays" of high resistance were used, and the strongest of nitric acid batteries, which became more portable as the war progressed. It was not long before the generals began to be surprised and delighted to find a wire strung and the operator ready, with his instrument on a cracker-box, at the end of a day's march. "No orders ever had to be given to set up the telegraph," said General Grant in his memoirs. It was always there, ready for the commander's orders, perhaps before he had his evening meal.

Wherever Richard O'Brien was in '62, you could be pretty sure of finding John not far off. When Union troops took over Norfolk in May, Richard was sent there, while John went to the railroad station at Suffolk, 20 miles to westward. The station was a mile from military headquarters, which, for some reason or other, was given no telegraph office. John had little trouble in keeping tabs on the two or three trains a day which ambled to and fro at irregular intervals, and he had a cavalryman as his dispatch-bearer to and from the Army headquarters. Fifty-nine-year-old General Mansfield, the commander of the unit there, rode over alone on horseback every three or four evenings, to see how John was getting along. "Everything all right?" he would ask. "Is your orderly satisfactory? Getting your rations regularly? Anybody giving you any trouble?" He would chat a while, maybe tell a story of his Mexican War experience, then say, "I must be getting back to camp. Good-night, John."

A little more than three months later, John wept again when he heard the news of the good old General's death on the bloody field of Antietam.

The War Department was moving ops every few weeks, like pawns on a chessboard, often for no apparent reason. "Somebody up there must be having fun," the boys used to say to each other. John O'Brien stayed at Suffolk no more than a month. Then Richard was shifted back to Fort Monroe, and John took his place at Norfolk, where he shared the twenty-four hours with an older man. They two were the liaison or relay men between Suffolk and Washington, having to repeat all messages. The trouble was that the War Office now and then, in one of its unexplainable moments, would send John's co-laborer somewhere else, and then it might be three or four days before a replacement came, which meant that John would have to work around the clock until then.

Bright younger boys like Billy Dealey and John O'Brien were feeling the lack of a formal education, and were trying to repair the oversight. Bill had gotten hold of a copy of Cobbert's Grammar, and after digging through it, with how much profit we do not know, had lent it to John. He in turn set out to *memorize* it, as a means of keeping himself awake on long night vigils. One would think it more apt to put him to sleep. But he had now discovered the dreamland of fiction, and paid more attention to that than to the grammar.

Once when he was on duty three days and nights in succession, taking naps only between calls with his head on his crossed hands on the table, he was reading a borrowed, dog-eared copy of *Ivanhoe* when he fell asleep about midnight. Eventually he became aware of his call being repeated close to his ear. He came drowsily awake, his right hand still asleep from its long cramped position. Clasping and unclasping his fingers, he finally answered the call.

68

"Wr U bn?" demanded Fortress Monroe, brusquely.

"Aslcep," admitted John.

"Wy didn't U acknowl 2 msgs just sent?" was the next query.

"I had no msgs," declared John.

"We called, U ans & we gave U 2 telegs, but U did not acknowl," insisted Monroe.

"Pls repeat," said John. "I don't remember them."

The messages were repeated, John wrote them down and relayed them to the Suffolk railroad station and Army headquarters. Then he looked at his *Ivanhoe,* lying almost under his hands. It was open at the point where dastardly Prince John, who was scheming to seize the English crown, received that frightening note, "Take care of thyself, for the Devil is unchained," meaning that his mighty brother, King Richard the Lion-Heart, was free from his Continental prison and on the way home. Now telegrapher John, in astonishment, saw pencil scrawls across both of the opened pages, mingling with the print. Looking closer, he found that those two messages had been written there in halting fashion and staggering script, sometimes straying off the edges, an occasional word omitted as well as one whole sentence.

He had actually received and written down the messages in his sleep.

VI

Wire Will-o-the-Wisps

An instance of how the War Department, under mistaken ideas as to what was going on in the field, tossed telegraph operators hither and yon like feathers in a gale, leaving them to do a deal of frenzied shifting for themselves, occurred in the early summer of 1862.

The Union Generals Fremont and Banks were in the Shenandoah Valley, each with a small army under him, and Washington had the mistaken notion that they controlled the area. The War Office was not yet acquainted with a fellow named Stonewall Jackson, who flitted about the Valley like a ghost, only he packed a punch such as few ghosts ever had. Fremont and Banks, who were no match for him as tacticians, had the impossible task of holding him in check. The War Department decided that all they needed was better telegraph service.

At that time, Thomas Q. Waterhouse and Charles W. Moore were operating an office near Manassas Junction, in a one-room shack just slightly larger than necessary to turn around in. In striking contrast to the situation around Fortress Monroe, here, where there was far less to do, there were ops for day and night shifts. A dry goods box held the telegraph instruments and was also the dining table. A nail keg with the only chair. The remains of an old stove, held together with telegraph wire, was the cooking apparatus; and a cheap coffin, whose acquisition, to say the best of it, had been highly irregular, served as a bed, whose chief difficulty was that one had to get out of it to turn over. As the ops took turns at sleeping in it, only one blanket was necessary, even in winter, and none at all now that the weather was growing warm. For such an establishment, a servant was of course needed, and this they had in the person of a colored youth known as Delaware, who did the cooking and dusted the furniture.

(Incidentally, a few weeks later, just before the Second Battle of Bull Run, Ed Conway operated from one of those pine boxes which are the outer casings of coffins, lying on the depot platform at Manassas Junction. He had his instrument hidden in it, and once, when an enemy detachment swarmed by, he himself hid in the box, drawing the lid over him carefully and trusting that the intruders wouldn't notice that it wasn't fastened or see the wire emerging from it. Having a dislike of coffins in principle, they stayed away from it, and incredibly enough, did not discover him.)

Well, Waterhouse and Moore were ordered to the Valley and a "special train," consisting of one ramshackle coach with some of the cane seats missing and drawn by a wheezy little locomotive, came by the Junction and picked them up. As they took their keys with them, their office was closed, and Delaware went back to his nearby farm home. Already on the train were Dick Graham, and Frank Lamb, who had been operating at Alexandria, and who spoke with a drawl which he could easily develop into a believable Virginia dialect. William McIntosh, an older man, a lineman, was also aboard, going to set up some new wires in the Valley, and some battery jars and carboys of acid completed the train's cargo. At another little station along the line, a fifth operator named Bickford joined them, on his way to join General Banks.

"Hey! Ain't we telegraphers something!" bawled Tom Waterhouse, standing in the aisle as the car rocked and bounced along. "Usually we have to walk, unless we can steal a ride on a caisson, and now they are hauling us in special trains."

"I miss the plush seats, though," quipped Graham.

"Write a complaint to ol' Ed Stanton about it," advised McIntosh. "Cuss him out."

Dick Graham didn't stay with them long; under orders, he dropped off at Thoroughfare Gap. The others jogged on as the day waned, exchanging facts and rumors about other ops whom they knew or didn't know. Henry Buell was with Banks, who had fallen back to Strasburg. A couple of other fellows named Hall and Lounsbury had been with Banks, but whether they were there still, no one could say. Didn't seem as if Banks would need three operators. Frank Drummond and Tom Armor were operating at Winchester, farther down the Valley. Jackson had whaled the

71

daylights out of Fremont at Cross Keys and Port Republic and a couple of other places, and was now heading for Banks with blood in his eye. He was hell on wheels, that fellow.

The Blue Ridge, just ahead of them, began to throw its long afternoon shadow over the train. They were to pass through it at Manassas Gap, just beyond which, in the edge of the Valley, was the village of Front Royal. They ate their sandwiches and whatever food they had been able to bring with them, and drank water out of the engine tank; a bit cindery, but it had to do. The train stopped frequently—for wood, for water, and wherever there was a telegraph office, for news, if any. Darkness fell as they stopped at a little station called Linden, and the engine crew heard that Jackson was approaching Front Royal.

"I dunno as I can git you boys in there," said the engineer. "They're liable to stop us any time, and I'll have to run slow from here, for fear they'll pile ties or somepn on the track and throw us off."

"Well, don't let us fall into the hands of the Johnnies if you can help it," urged Charlie Moore. "We'll wind up in Libby Prison if you do. They look on us as being the same as soldiers."

Half an hour later, the train, which was creeping over the curving miles into the rugged Gap, suddenly came to a jarring stop as the engineer reversed and spun his wheels backward, throwing two or three passengers from their seats and awakening some others from sleep. The fireman, who had been at the rear end of the tender, shifting his stock of wood, took a look forward at slouch-hatted soldiers around a campfire and two standing on the track with guns aport, then dropped over the tail-end of the tender to the front platform of the coach, opened the door and hissed in a loud whisper;—

"S-st! Graycoats ahead. Slip out the back door if you wanta git away."

They lost no time. The one piece of candle which had been burning in the front end of the car was just guttering out, leaving the car in darkness. Each grabbed his instrument and his handbag, if he was plutocratic enough to have one, and ran to the rear door. They tried to tiptoe down the steps, four of them on one side, Waterhouse on the other, with no fixed purpose as to which way to go after they reached the ground. Waterhouse, not knowing that he was the only one who came down on that side,

72

started running along the path outside the tie-ends, back in the direction from which they had come. He was muttering, "This way! This way!" and did not discover until he had run some distance that no one was following him. He presently stumbled and fell with his chest across a tie-end and got such a shaking-up that he crouched, gasping, for a few seconds. Looking back, he could get no clear idea of what was going on, but did not believe the soldiers had captured his comrades. It would have been too dangerous to try to contact them now. It was every man for himself now; he decided to go back along the railroad to Rectortown, some 25 miles away, where Ed Conway was operating for General Geary. After a sleep of several hours on the platform of a little station, he pushed on, reaching Rectortown in the afternoon of the next day, covered with mud. Ed welcomed him, gave him some food and a cot ("But take those muddy clothes off before you lie down on it") and he was snoozing peacefully when Ed shook him and said, "Get up, Tom. We're retreating;" and so he passes out of this episode.

The four others had instinctively run down the steps on the north side of the car, away from Rebel territory, and scrambled up a slope, tormented with rocks and scrub, warning each other in whispers, "Don't make any noise, thrashing through the bushes." At last, when they were out of breath, they came to a big rock which rose straight from the ground, and sat down in a row, leaning their backs against it gratefully. For some moments they did nothing but breathe hard. Then someone asked, "Everybody got his key?"

Everybody had. "What'll we do now?" was the next whisper.

"I gotta get to Strasburg," said Bickford. "General Banks' headquarters are at Strasburg. I'm ordered to join him there."

"Where is Strasburg?" asked someone. There was a moment of silence. Nobody knew.

"It's on the railroad," continued Bickford. "I expected to go there by rail. Didn't know I'd have to walk."

"Might as well make up your mind," said McIntosh, "that from here on, wherever you go, you'll walk."

Charlie Moore had been growing excited. "Hey! There's only four of us here," he exclaimed. "This is Mac, next to me, and Frank Lamb, and Bick—where's Tom? Tom's gone!" His voice had risen, bringing a chorus of "Sh-h-h!"

"I'll swear he came out of the car," said Lamb. "He was in the aisle, right ahead of me."

"Come to think of it," said McIntosh, "somebody got off on the other side of the car from us. Musta been Waterhouse."

"But that was the rebel side of the track," protested Charlie. "Where could he've gone?"

"Oh, he can take care of himself, I guess," soothed McIntosh.

"He'll get caught, sure as God made little apples," declared Charlie.

But there was nothing they could do about Tom, so they talked on in low tones, agreeing that they must obey orders and get over into the Valley somehow, but that they would have to wait for daylight before they made any move. One by one they grew drowsy and fell into troubled sleep.

Someone was awake as the first pink of dawn tinged the East, and aroused the others. Looking around them, they found that they were in a complex of steep little wooded knobs into which the Blue Ridge had somehow been broken to form Manassas Gap. The railroad crept through the lowest notch of it. Someone wondered how far it was to Front Royal. It was four or five miles, but none of them knew that. The railroad was partly screened from them by trees and bushes, but Charlie crawled down to a better viewpoint, and discovered that their special train had been taken away while they slept.

"I could still see soldiers figurin' around down there, though," he said. "I think we better keep outa sight of the railroad."

"But work westward," amended McIntosh.

"I gotta get to Strasburg." Bick never lost sight of that for a moment.

So they set forth, keeping back from the railroad, and with the rising sun usually at their backs. Sometimes they were just plunging through the woods, where the underbrush was scanty on the rocky hillsides, sometimes they followed dim, mysterious little near-paths which seemed to begin and end nowhere; cow-paths, Lamb said they were; "old cow-paths, though the cows are all gone now." And presently they rounded a turn and saw just below them a pretty little cove, a hidden valley, tucked away among the hills, which rose all around it, for the brook which made it left the valley by a right-angled bend, with the hill beyond folding it in; and there in the cove was a well-tended little farm, with a log dwelling

74

and a small log barn. The fugitives, hovering in the edge of the woods, saw some Negro children playing about the yard, and a Negro man going to the barn, perhaps to feed a mule or cow.

"Wonder if we could get anything to eat from that man," said someone, voicing the thought of all of them.

"Queer, his living here, independent-like," said Lamb. In Virginia, Negroes were usually slaves.

"He's apt to be on our side, if we can make him believe we're Yankee," remarked McIntosh.

They debated whether one of them should approach him as an emissary while the rest stayed in hiding, but decided that it would be better that they all go at once. The man was obviously much startled when he first saw them coming. While the children ran and hid behind the house, he stood motionless, watching them with a mixture of alarm and resignation in his countenance. Perhaps as they neared him and he saw how young they were—McIntosh was only in his late twenties—and that they were not in uniform, he relaxed a little.

They had decided to be frank. "We are telegraphers with the Union Army," said McIntosh. "Do you know what a telegrapher is?"

Yassuh, he knew. McIntosh explained their escape from the train, and asked, "Have you anything to eat that you'd sell us? We'll pay you for it in good United States silver money."

Glancing at his wife, who had come to the door of the cabin, he said that he thought there might be some cold vegetables and corn pone left over from last night, and she could fry some meat . . . "But they ain't no coffee," he warned.

"All right, we'll have to get along without coffee," they said. In a few minutes they were seated on a bench outside the house door, devouring food that was coarse but sustaining.

The Negro's apparently independent status intrigued the boys. "How do you happen to be living out here?" one of them asked.

"I's a freedman," he replied, standing straight, with pride in his bearing and voice. "I got my paper in de house. Cain't nobody order me around, not rightly."

They congratulated him. "But do these Rebel soldiers respect your papers?" asked McIntosh.

"Ain't no sojers ever found me yit, hid away in dis little valley like I is," he answered with a grin. "I has nearly all my dealin's wid a little cross-roads sto', an' hardly ever goes into Front Royal. An' please, young mahsters, don't tell anybody about me bein' heah. Ef de sojers ever found me, Yank or Reb, dey'd take ev-ything I got; an' ef 'twas de Confedicks, dey'd th'ow me back into chains."

"Don't worry," they told him. "We won't mention you. We're trusting you, and you may trust us."

"Which way is Strasburg?" asked Bickford.

"Nigh as I can tell, it's sorta dataway," he pointed westward. "How far I dunno."

"And Winchester's up this way, isn't it?" asked Moore, pointing to the north.

"Yassuh. But y'all gotta cross de rivah—"

"What river?"

"De Shenando'. You could cross by de railroad bridge, 'bout a mile from Front Rayol, but dey may be Confedick sojers dar now. But dis side de bridge, maybe three mile downstream is a fo'd, whar you kin wade across. 'Twon't be mo'n two, three feet deep now. Or dey's a man lives nigh de fo'd dat'll set y'all across in a boat—ef you ain't afraid to trust him."

In parting, they gave him a half-dollar—a coin with a much greater purchasing power then than now—and he was well content. Following a path down the brook, they made a turn to the right, and the little valley vanished as if it had never been. More and more windings followed, and suddenly the hills fell away and a broad, gently sloping land lay before them—the Shenandoah Valley.

And now they began to hear firing to southwestward; a rattle of musketry, increasing in volume, and occasionaly punctuated by cannon-shot. It was Colonel Kenly's small detachment of Banks's army, being thrashed at Front Royal by Jackson, with the result that the greater part of his force were taken prisoners.

"That don't sound good," said McIntosh. "We'd better be makin' tracks down the Valley towards the Potomac."

"I gotta get to Strasburg," Bick reminded him.

They pushed across fields, trying to keep out of sight of farmhouses; reached the road that evidently led to the ford, and skulked along its sides, looking sharply in all directions, dodging into the bushes if they saw anybody. Behind them, the battle rumbled on. At length the river came in sight.

"That must be the house of the man who would row us across," said McIntosh, pointing. "Shall we risk it, boys?"

"No!" exclaimed Charlie, vehemently. "I wouldn't trust him. He's probably a rebel. We'd just be walking into a trap. I'd rather wade across, even if I have to swim. In this hot sun, our clothes will dry in a little while."

The others were of the same mind. They went down to the edge of the clear, tranquil stream, undressed from the waist down and holding their clothes high, waded across. Even on the shortest of them, it was only waist deep.

As they sat, putting on their shoes on the farther shore, Bickford said, "I'm turning west here, towards Strasburg. You fellows going with me? It can't be more than five or six miles."

He and McIntosh had already had some argument about this since they left the train, and now McIntosh broke out again.

"Listen, Bick," he said, "I think you're makin' a bad mistake. You're gointa try to cross right across the front of Jackson's army, and him movin' this way, and fast. He's already brushed Fremont aside like a fly, and this small-caliber politician Banks can't even slow him up. We can't any of us reach the posts we were ordered to go to, and we can't be blamed if we head back towards the Potomac; get out of the mess the best way we can. It won't do the Government any good for us to fall into a Rebel prison, just from some damfool, bullheaded notion that we've gotta go where they told us to go, whether the Confederate army likes it or not."

Moore and Lamb added their remonstrances, but Bickford was adamant.

"Strasburg is my destination," he said, rising to his feet, "and I've got to hurry. Good-bye, boys, and good luck. See you at Harper's Ferry—maybe."

He climbed a fence and struck off along the edge of a field of young wheat. The others moved northward along the road for some time without saying a word. Then Charlie Moore spoke.

"Well, there goes another of us," he said. "First, Tom Waterhouse, and now Bick. I wish to goodness I knew what has happened to Tom."

"You might not like it if you knew," observed McIntosh.

Buoyed up by a solid even if uncouth breakfast under their belts, they strode along in good style for four or five miles, seeing almost nobody and meeting no vehicles. With the war so close to

77

their doors, people were not venturing away from their homes. At length they became aware of distant firing, far away to westward.

"There's Jackson attacking Banks at Strasburg," said McIntosh. "I bet old Bick wishes he was with us now," said Lamb. "They'll get him, sure as the world."

"Looky yonder. What's that?" exclaimed Moore.

Their road had been parallelling the railroad that ran north through Front Royal to Hagerstown—usually a mile or more or less from it. Now Charlie was pointing to a group of men, so far away that they looked little bigger than ants, who appeared to be tearing up the track.

"What are they, Union or Rebs?" asked someone.

They were too far away to identify. "Must be Union," was McIntosh's opinion. "The Rebs wouldn't be wrecking the track in front of themselves. This must be Union men trying to slow up tthe Johnnies."

"Here comes somebody behind us, too," was the next cry. They were on fairly high ground, and looking back a mile or two, what seemed to be cavalry were visible, raising a cloud of dust.

"Off the road!" They skittered up a slope to their right and lay flat in a sassafras thicket. "That may be our own men," said McIntosh, "but let's take no chances until we see the color of their uniforms."

They lay there, muttering to each other and vainly awaiting the clatter of hoofs, for more than half an hour. Then Lamb crept forth and reported that the cavalry had disappeared, but that he thought he could trace the remains of the dust-cloud going westward on a cross-road. The rail-wreckers had disappeared, too, and woodlands to north and south of where they had been made it impossible to decide which way they had gone.

The trio now took to the road again, nervous as cats, frequently looking behind them, and becoming painfully aware that it had been several hours since they enjoyed that peaceful breakfast in that little sylvan valley. But they were in hostile country now, and they dared not ask for food at a farmhouse lest they betray themselves. They still met no vehicles on the road. People peered curiously at them from the houses they passed, but said nothing. They had trudged another two miles or more when Charlie looked back and exclaimed, "More troopers!" The others whirled for a look.

"Over that wall, boys," cried McIntosh. The three slid over a rough stone fence which bordered the field at their left—keeping themselves as flat as possible, so as not to bulk too large in the landscape—and lay close to the base of the wall on the other side as the cavalry thundered by a few minutes later. Raising their heads as the sounds receded, they saw that the horsemen were indeed graycoats.

"I think I see infantry far back there, too," said Charlie, whose eyes were keen.

"We'd better take to the railroad," thought Lamb. "This road is getting too crowded."

They plunged hurriedly through weedy old fields and woods to the railroad, saw no soldiers thereon, either way, but did see them moving northward on parallel roads. The sounds of the skirmish to westward had thinned out to scattering shots.

"Looks as if we're right in the midst of the Reb army," said Moore.

"Maybe Bick had the right idea, after all," gloomed Frank. "Maybe he's safe under Banks's wing right now."

"And with plenty to eat," added Charlie, voicing the thought which nagged at the consciousness of all of them.

Where a dim road wriggled across the track, a lank, loosely assembled, hollow-jawed, barefoot rustic, shuffling through the dust in a floppy hat and cottonade breeches precariously sustained by a single cotton gallus, paused to survey the strangers, his jaws working rhythmically on a huge cud of tobacco. Frank Lamb, the Southern impersonator, accosted him as spokesman.

"Howdy, friend," said he. "You know anything about wheah Gen'l Imboden's headquahtehs might be?"

"Naw," was the reply. "Y'all ahmy men?"

"Confed'ate telegraphehs," drawled Frank. "We got separated from ouah commands durin' the fightin' at Front Royal today, and we ah tryin' to ketch up. How fah is Winchesteh from heah?"

He shook his head, and spurted a half-pint of tobacco juice on the track before revealing, "This heah railroad don't go thoo Winchesteh."

That was a jolt, but Frank was quick-witted enough to take it with seeming indifference. "We don't wanta to go theah nohow," he said. "Not right away, that is. The Yanks ah still theah, but

Stonewall said he'd be theah by this evenin'. Who I right now wanta find is Gin'l Imboden. Well, good-day, strangeh."

They left him, standing, staring after them, his jaws still chomp, chomp, chomping on that wad of tobacco. Whether he believed Frank's yarn or not was doubtful.

"I don't like that fellow's looks," said Charlie.

"Who could?" countered Frank.

"He suspects us, and he'll probably run and tell somebody about us."

"I can't imagine him running anywhere," quipped McIntosh. "The only part of his body that'll ever work hard is his jaws. But boys, forget about him. We're in a trap. My idea is that we better leave the railroad and work west or northwest until we get in contact with Banks's men. We can keep our course by the sun; but we better stay in the woods as much as possible and not talk to anybody."

They did just that—prowling in the shadows wherever they could, peeping out of every covert before they ventured to cross an open space. They saw plenty of evidence that Confederates were taking over the area, and they gave every such unit a wide berth. Unluckily, as the afternoon wore on, clouds obscured the sun, though McIntosh claimed to be holding the course—whenever they were in the woods—by the moss on the tree-trunks.

The clouds thickened and the air became heavier. At dusk, they were in sight of a Confederate camp, and circled widely around it in the gathering darkness. When they finally bumped up against a fence and paused, even McIntosh had to admit that he didn't know which was north and which was west. Stumbling, they crept a little way along the fence, and became aware of some small buildings, which they quickly identified as the slave quarters of a plantation. There were no lights to be seen in any of them, and as it was still comparatively early in the evening, it was reasonable to suppose that not everybody would have gone to bed. But they heard no snores anywhere. There was only one conclusion; the cabins were empty—deserted.

"Slaves all sloped north," whispered one of the boys.

They tried one of the doors. It swung open readily. Stepping inside, one of them lighted a match. There was a bed in the room, on which was a shuck mattress, but no covers. There were two or three split-bottomed chairs, but nothing else.

Army of the Potomac operators in August, 1864. Still no uniforms, but some had raised whiskers.

Some operators in the Gettysburg campaign. The youth leaning against the tentpole was A. Harper Caldwell, chief operator of the Army of the Potomac.

"This is a godsend," said someone. "It's gointa rain tonight, and I wanta sleep under a roof."

"I'll sleep on the floor," said Charlie. "I wouldn't lie down on that bed for a ten-dollar bill. The bugs would carry a fellow off bodily before morning."

The sentiments of the others were similar, and they were unamimous in their lamentations for the pains of hunger. "We've just gotta scrabble some grub in the morning," said McIntosh, "steal it if we can, or we can't go on. Maybe we can find a nigger that'll help us."

"If I only had another drink from that good spring we passed this afternoon—" mourned Charlie.

"Shut up!" snapped Mac, "and let's get some sleep. We've prob'ly got a hard day before us tomorrow."

They sprawled on the rough floor, where weariness from their long day's hike finally overcame the pains of their empty bellies, and they slept a drugged sleep. Even a thunderstorm in the latter part of the night passed unnoticed by them. The new day dawned, the sun rose, and still they slept. Then suddenly Frank Lamb and Charlie Moore, who lay on either side of McIntosh, felt themselves poked harshly in the ribs. They opened their eyes upon the unwelcome sight of two soldiers, one of them grim-faced, the other grinning, whose gun-muzzles had just punched them awake. Between the soldiers stood a handsome, middle-aged gentleman of the Southern planter type, with graying hair and mustache, negligently handling a pistol.

"Spies, eh?" said the gentleman, as the three refugees sat up in alarm.

"No, suh," protested Frank, holding up his instrument. "We ah telegraphehs—Confed'ate teleg—"

"Don't try any of that bogus dialect on me," snapped the gentleman. "It's as spurious as a wig. You've got Yankee written all over you. Stand up!"

They rose to their feet. "Take that man's pistol," said their captor, pointing to McIntosh, the only one who was so armed. "See if the others have any."

"No, sir, Colonel," said one of the soldiers, after a quick frisking. "What'll we do with 'em, Colonel?"

"I would suggest that you throw them in your nearest guardhouse, and mix 'em with the prisoners you take today."

McIntosh spoke up. "We'll surrender, Colonel," said be, "if you'll give us breakfast—anything to eat."

The Colonel was amused. "Oh, you will, will you?" he retorted. "That's a fair offer, I must say."

"We haven't had anything to eat for twenty-four hours, Colonel," pleaded Charlie. "We're nearly starved."

His boyish, pleading face evidently touched the gentleman. "Well, I'm not inhuman," he said, "Take them to the kitchen and tell the cook to give them breakfast. Eat a plenty," he admonished the boys. "I am told that the menu in Libby Prison is not what you'd call Lucullan."

They didn't know what that meant, but they knew what Libby Prison was. "But we're not soldiers, sir," objected McIntosh. "We're civilians, not military men."

"Nevertheless, you're working for the military," retorted the gentleman. "What do you expect us to do? Turn you loose, so you can go back to work for your army again? No, no, that won't wash."

He turned away, and the soldiers nudged the three towards the kitchen of the "big house," a pretentious mansion in Colonial style. They did not need much urging, as the fragrance of coffee and frying meat reached their nostrils. When McIntosh meditated gloomily, "Well, this is the end of the road," Charlie rejoined, "Right now, I'm not sorry." If he could have guessed what was before him, he would not have said that.

The story here was the same as on many another plantation. The field hands, as many of them as could manage it, had slipped away northward in search of freedom, while the house servants, closer to the white family and living an easier life, remained loyal. The cook, a competent black woman, looked rather scornfully at the unkempt trio ushered into her immaculate kitchen, but she softened a little when Charlie exclaimed enthusiastically, "Gosh, cook, this is the best food I ever ate." Presently she was asking, "Have some mo' coffee. It's real coffee."

That was the last real meal that any of them ate for months thereafter.

Bickford had indeed been the lucky one. Driving westward he encountered the outskirts of Banks's retreating army, and went with it to Winchester. There was no longer a job for him in the Valley, for Jackson was systematically clearing out the Union troops there. At the railroad station in Winchester Frank Drummond and Tom Armor had been working around the clock as relay operators between the generals in the Valley and Washington. They were pretty tired when Banks fell back to that place and on the day after Bickford joined him, was pummeled again by Jackson.

As it became evident to Banks that defeat was again his portion, Drummond sent to Washington the general's telegram, revealing that he was falling back again, this time to the Potomac. That message had much to do with deciding the course of the yet-to-come Seven Days' Battles, four weeks and 150 miles away. General McDowell, who, with 40,000 men, had been ordered to march to reinforce McClellan on his right, was hastily recalled by the frightened Administration to defend Washington from this demon Jackson—who really had no designs on the Capital at all, but was going to Richmond to reinforce Lee as soon as he had mopped up the Valley. Thus Jackson was unhindered as he made one of his lightning marches to strike McClellan's outnumbered right wing at Gaines's Mill, on June 27th.

The battle was raging in the outskirts of Winchester when a staff officer said to Drummond, "We'll take Armor with us, to cut in on the wire if possible, and you stay here to handle rearguard business. I've assigned you two mounted orderlies and a saddled horse for your own use, so you can make a quick escape at the last moment." Frank nodded as he hammered the key.

"Shall I stay with you?" asked Bickford.

"No, you're on foot. Go ahead with the troops. I'll be along a little later." He wished he could be sure of that.

Nearer and nearer the sound of battle. Frank was sending Banks's last message, which was unnecessarily wordy. Nearer—nearer; now he could faintly hear the rebel yell.

"See if my horse is ready," he said to an orderly.

"Right in front of the door," was the answer, "with the bridle throwed over the hitchin' post."

"Well, you boys clear out," he told the orderlies. "I won't need you any more. Join your command."

They promptly vanished, and galloped away. The crackle of musketry and the yells were terribly near. Retreating Yankee soldiers were running past the station. Frank was standing, ticking off the final words; his dispatch copies were in his pocket. At that moment a clatter of hoofs, a scouring of gravel as a horse was pulled up suddenly, and a sweating orderly rushed in, thrusting a crumpled paper at Frank.

"From General Banks. Rush." He whirled and was gone.

Incompetent Banks wanted reinforcements sent from Harper's Ferry to help slow up the enemy and save him and his command from annihilation. Frank felt a flush of anger cover his whole body as his blood pressure rose into the hundreds. Why didn't Banks have Armor or Bickford cut in on the wire to Harper's Ferry instead of calling on him to stay and continue working, with the enemy almost on top of him? But on second thought, maybe Banks wasn't following the wire to the Ferry. Anyhow, duty was duty, so he began trying to call Harper's Ferry, to get a wire open to Washington. "HF, HF HF" he ticked—now he could see the Johnnies coming, far down the street—"HF, HF, HF!" But Harper's Ferry was busy on the Washington wire, and either refused to be bothered or didn't realize the desperate, perhaps tragic, importance of a few seconds' delay. "HF, HF, HF!"—but still that maddening repudiation! Scarcely knowing what he did, he ran to the door for a look at his horse. It was gone! Some frightened soldier had vaulted into the saddle and fled with it. In a muddle of Union infantry down the street, he saw some trying to rally, some fleeing outright, throwing away equipment as they ran. On the other side of the station, the Rebs were within fifty yards of him, dog-trotting cautiously. Frank leaped back to his key and tried "HF, HF" again, meanwhile pulling his dispatches from his pocket with his left hand, tossing them on the table and striking a match to them. Harper's Ferry still ignored him; after all, he'd been nagging it only three or four minutes, though it seemed hours—and now he gave it up. Snatching his instrument from the table and dashing out the door, he thought to dodge into a side street and vanish among buildings. But as he turned into the cross-street, he met Confederate cavalry, head-on. Raising his instrument high in air, he dashed it with all his force against the stone pavement and stepped on it, ruining it beyond repair. As he whirled to dart through a yard, a trooper's pistol muzzle halted him; and completely spent, he relaxed and raised his empty hands. He had done his best and it had taken a little too long.

He was reported in the news dispatches as killed; a soldier said he saw him fall.

General Banks succeeded in getting back to Harper's Ferry with a whole skin, though many of his men did not. Jackson was content to let him rest there, while he went back to deal Fremont a few more blows before going to the aid of General Lee.

Frank Drummond now began to experience the rigors of war captivity. After a night's uneasy rest, he, in company with other prisoners, started trudging southward, away from any Yankee threat, the intent of his captors being to make a detour via the upper Valley around the battle area, and approach Richmond and Libby Prison from the southwest. On the second day of march, the 700 of Colonel Kenly's men captured at Front Royal were added to the cavalcade, and Frank quickly discovered four other telegraph prisoners, too, our three friends, Moore, McIntosh, as well as Henry Buell, who had been with Banks at Strasburg, but who, like Frank, had been left behind, cut off and captured

"Know what became of Bickford?" asked one of the trio of wanderers.

"Last I saw of him," replied Frank, "he was making strides about eight feet long towards the Potomac. I have an idea that Banks outran Jackson. I haven't seen anything of Armor or Bickford, so I guess they got away."

Frank kept a diary during his captivity, which reveals the toughness of the war prisoners' lot. The Confederacy was already having a shortage of food, and war prisoners were of course the first to be stinted. On May 31st they started their march at 12:30 p.m. "Marched 15 miles," says the diary, "and halted for night in middle of road. Soldiers would not allow us into field close by, so we were compelled to lie down in mud so deep that Lieut. Rice of the 5th Connecticut, with whom I slept, could not see a particle of his blanket when we got up, and so left it there; and I can say that he regretted leaving it for months afterward. It rained very heavily all night. We arose from our soft bed soaking wet, cold, hungry and very miserable. Marched at 5 a.m. for Strasburg. Here the officers got breakfast at hotels, for which they paid." (Marched again) "Halted at 4 p.m. 11 miles from Strasburg, and prospects were held out that we would get half rations, uncooked, which proved true, for each received 4 crackers (hard tack) . . . June 2, marched 15 miles to Mt. Jackson . . . June 3, marched 16 miles. Officers camped in a dirty barn. Very hot. No rations.

After all were lying, tired and quiet, I sang very loudly the 'Bacon and Greens' song:

> Oh, there's charm in this dish, rightly taken,
> Than from custards and jellies an epicure weans,
> Stick your fork in the fat, wrap your greens round the bacon,
> And you'll vow there's no dish like good bacon and greens.

Cries of "Shut up!" "Gag him" "Put him out!" greeted the rendition of this ditty. Next day, June 4th, they marched 17 miles to Harrisonburg. "No rations. Feet very sore. Camped in field near depot." Here Frank was near enough a store to buy some provisions, which he divided with his fellow-telegraphers. The prisoners' pocket money had not been taken from them; except on the rarest of occasions, that wasn't done in Civil War America; and Drummond, in the early stages of the march, was pretty well heeled. Two days later, after another long march without rations, "Rained very fast all morning. Sun came out at noon. Went to town with guard; bought shoes, towels and soap. Washed in river, put up tent, received rations and slept well." But next day Charlie Moore was very ill—the first of two illnesses he suffered —and had to travel by wagon. Between illnesses and when he had had something to eat, he could outjump any of them. On June 9 he records, "Rations of fat pork, no bread. Marched 16 miles to North Garden Station. Changed our quarters in the midst of a heavy rain to a worse one." Next day they were loaded in box cars and taken by rail to Lynchburg.

At that city they were marched to the Fair Grounds and rations were served out. Buell was ill and Drummond didn't feel so well. But they rigged up a sleeping place in the cattle sheds, with boards to lie on, and at least were "in the dry." Drummond bought $17 worth of food and now they had better rest and felt better, though the rations were always watery soup, stringy boiled beef and bread; they never varied. One evening they had a womanless dance in one of the Fair buildings to the music of some prisoner's flute.

On August 1st another op joined them—Marion Kerner, who had been picked up in the Valley. He brought another of the rumors which had been swirling about at times all through the march, namely, that they were soon to be paroled. But it never happened, and they continued to stagnate there in the Fair Ground. Drummond changed his last "big money," a ten-dollar gold piece, for paper money, receiving $15 for it, one-third in Confederate and two-thirds on Union paper.

There was "something wrong" with the well in the Fair Ground which was their water supply, and for a long time they got only half-portions of water, presumably on the theory that a little bad water wouldn't hurt them as much as a lot. Parole rumors persisted, but they were told that if they wanted to be exchanged, they would have to provide their own exchanges, which was manifestly impossible. After two months at the Lynchburg prison camp, they were again herded into box cars and taken to the old tobacco warehouse in Richmond which had become Libby Prison. A long month there in squalor, hunger and boredom, and then came the welcome word, "Parole!"

On September 14th the list of names of those who were to go home was read. All the operators were there except Charlie Moore. It was like a blow in the face to him.

"I wonder why I'm not called," he said, almost in tears. "What have I done to offend the powers that be?"

"There must be some mistake," was Frank Drummond's opinion. He went to the commandant and said, "Sir, you have all the telegraph operators except Charles W. Moore listed for parole. Is there any reason why he is omitted? Seems to me he's on the same basis as the rest of us."

The major at first said impatiently that there had been no mistake, but upon Drummond's urging, he checked again and found that Moore's name had indeed been overlooked. So Charlie was made happy again and prepared—no, there wasn't any particular preparing to do, as none of them had any baggage—to go home. They were taken by rail down to tidewater, then by boat to Annapolis, and by rail to Washington. They were "heartily welcomed" says Frank at the War department, "though we were a hard looking lot, and it was unsafe to come too near us. We got some money, and I got permission for Tommy Armor to accompany me to procure an entire change of wardrobe. I stood in the middle of the floor and directed the purchase from a safe distance, then made for the nearest bath-house, rolled all my clothes in a bundle, and for obvious reasons, threw them out the back window."

And so ended the Odyssey.

VII

Bunnell on the Job

Late in June, 1862, the Federal Army of the Potomac, under General McClellan, had moved up the Virginia Peninsula, between the York and James Rivers, in a drive towards Richmond. It moved on both sides of the swampy little Chickahominy River, General Porter's corps being on the north side of the swamp, the rest of the army on the south side. McClellan was hoping that Porter would be joined by 40,000 men under General McDowell, moving from the direction of Washington.*

On June 25th the Confederate army under General Lee moved to strike back at the invaders, and thus began the Seven Days' Battles. The first assaults were on Porter's corps. On the second day there was a brief but fierce battle in the afternoon along the glen of Beaver Dam Creek, which ended with the Confederates being repulsed. Now at nightfall it was over, but they were still out there, a mile beyond the creek, watching and waiting, their next move a mystery. General McClellan, the supreme commander, whose headquarters were on the other side of the Chickahominy, ten mile away, had ridden over with some of his staff, to join General Porter during the engagement. After it, he remained for discussion, Jesse Bunnell, Porter's telegraph operator, in his tiny tent alongside the General's, had his hands full, keeping the

---

*The Chicago Tribune, on January 30th, 1862, carried a few lines regarding the army telegraph, calling it "the most efficient department in the whole army," but adding a statement which must have been dreamed up by a staff writer in the city room, who had never been near the front; "The operators travel in large wagons with sleeping berths, tents and telegraphic equipment." As will be seen by the text of the accompanying chapter, the telegraphers, though indispensable, were, at least for the first two years of the war, the Cinderellas of the army.

top commander in touch with his own headquarters, and through it, with his other corps and division commanders south of the Chickahominy.

At eighteen, Jesse was already a veteran telegrapher. He had begun at eleven as a messenger boy in his home town of Massillon, Ohio, and two years later as an operator. He had three more winters in school, meanwhile continuing his key-pounding, then was a railroad telegrapher at various places in Ohio. He became noted for his speed in sending and receiving. In December, 1860, at seventeen, he made a two-hour record of 38 words per minute—and there were some pretty long words in that document, too—in sending President Buchanan's last Congressional message from Pittsburgh to Cincinnati, where it was received by L. C. Weir, another speed demon (later President of the Adams Express Company) without a break. When the war began, Jesse joined the Army Telegraph Corps.

Now in Porter's tent, well back from the lip of the deadly battle ravine, the two generals, close friends since their West Point days, sat down to talk after the end of the fray. Once Jesse heard McClellan's voice raised slightly in bitter vexation, saying, "As I feared, I am not going to get the help of McDowell's corps. The Administration is too fearful for its own skin to let him get out of sight. So he is being kept up there to guard Washington—against what? Against Stonewall Jackson, whereas I believe that Jackson is moving around to your right, aiming to help crush my army if possible."

Dusk deepened into darkness and still the talk went on, hour after hour, as Porter's various division and brigade commanders—Morell, Sykes, McCall, Reynolds, Griffin, Seymour, Meade, Martindale—dropped in to discuss today's happenings and tomorrow's possibilities with their chief and the top commander. Jesse ate a hasty supper of beans, bread and coffee from his left hand while he hammered the key or wrote incoming dispatches with his right, by the light of a candle stuck to a cracker box by its own fat. The periodic exchange of low-toned phrases between sentries, the occasional distant scream or wail of a wounded man being carried to the hospital tents, from which a faint glow might be seen through the trees, were the only punctuations of the constant small ticking of the telegraph, the buzz of conversation in the general's tent and the almost inaudible whispering rustle which

89

signified that all around, thousands of weary men lay, most of them asleep, sprawled on the ground in the warm June night with their arms beside them. Meanwhile Nature, ignoring the little bickerings of men, carried on as usual; the great dome of stars overhead twinkled peacefully; in wood and field the crickets, tree-toads, all the little musicians of the night, fifed and fiddled, as if they had forgotten the roar and crash of battle which had shaken the earth under them that afternoon. As Jesse fingered his key, he could hear a little screech-owl quavering—sounded as if it were in the tree right over his tent.

"I must choose between two courses of action," General McClellan was saying, "depending on what we hear about Jackson. Operator—" raising his voice, "is any news coming in at the moment."

"No, sir," replied Jesse.

"Well, here we are on the horns of a dilemma," the General continued. "If Jackson isn't slinking around to north and northeast of you, you will stay here and expect another clash tomorrow. If we hear that he's trying a flank movement, you will move to high ground east of here a few miles—" his finger traced a line of defense on a map over which the huddle of heads bent, while an aide held a candle nearer "—protecting the bridges by which you must retreat across the Chickahominy." General Barnard, chief engineer officer, who had drawn the map, took up the story there, his finger following a road past the farmhouse of a Dr. Gaines and a big grist mill that he owned, a mile away on Powhite Creek and a little hamlet known as Cold Harbor—"though where they get that 'harbor' I can't imagine," laughed Barnard. "It's not anywhere deep enough to float a skiff."

So the talk droned on until one a.m., and Jesse, who had been awake most of the night before, was almost dying of sleepiness when General McClellan and his aides finally took their leave, to ride back to his headquarters by starlight. "I'll call you the moment I hear anything definite," said the General as he shook hands with Porter. "Good-night, old fellow."

"Keep an ear on the wire, Bunnell," ordered General Porter, and sat down to write notes to certain under-commanders who had not been present at the conference, alerting them to the possible change of position. At times like these, sleep was supposed to be dispensed with; it was the last consideration; but there was a

90

limit to the endurance of the human body. Jesse heard the General saying "Order all possible baggage and equipment loaded in the wagons, ready to move—" and then he passed out, his head on his crossed arms on the cracker box beside his instrument, almost literally obeying the General's order to keep his ear on the wire.

Some time later he was awake briefly when the wire chattered, but it was only Charlie Jacques—whose touch on the key was as easily recognizeable as his voice would have been—at General Franklin's headquarters, reporting a story brought in by an alleged deserter. Snores from the adjacent darkened tents told that General Porter and his staff were snatching a nap. Within three minutes Jesse sank into slumber again, and this time it was profound.

Some time long afterward, he seemed to be gliding bodily at high speed along a wire through the forest, something clicking "FJ" every time he passed a pole with a jerk. Suddenly his eyelids flew open—he awoke; the instrument was giving his own call. His candle was burnt out, but his finger fell readily on the key and he answered.

"Where U been?" asked the wire in the smooth, swift enunciation of Harper Caldwell, General McClellan's operator.

"Asleep," admitted Jesse. Harp would understand; probably been asleep himself only a minute ago. "Waitl I lit a candle." He had one ready, lying beside the box. He scratched a match. "GA" (Go ahead) he directed, then with candle in his left hand, snatched out a pencil and wrote.

"To General Porter from the Commander," said the wire. Already Jesse was shouting, "General Porter! General Porter!"

"Yes," came the General's voice, still muffled by sleep, "What is it?"

"Message from General McClellan," replied Jesse, scribbling away. "It's the order to move."

An increasing stir was heard in all nearby tents. Matches were scratching, candles being lighted. The general hurried into Jesse's tent, he had to crouch to get into it, and on one knee he looked over Jesse's shoulder as he wrote out the orders, "Move at once to position discussed tonight. The commanding general has definite word that Jackson is moving to north and northeast of you. He must not flank you . . . " and so the dispatch went on for several sentences more. Meanwhile. the General was calling to his aides, telling them to send the order to the division commanders, who in turn would pass it to brigadiers. At the end of the dispatch, Porter said, "Acknowledge. The order will be executed as rapidly as possible. Hold hard, Bunnell; I'll be wanting to send another dispatch."

He rushed back to his tent, which was already being taken down, and in another five minutes was packed into a wagon, but the General scribbled a message by candlelight on a cracker box. The whole area had been in a bustle for several minutes—saddling and harnessing horses, striking and packing tents and cots; and now, marvelously, the clunk of wheels of loaded wagons began.

General Porter thrust a paper at Jesse with several hastily scrawled sentences on it—much too much of it, Jesse thought, but the General was incurably wordy. Jesse ran an eye over it, and had to halt the General with a foot in the stirrup to ask, "What is this word, sir? . . . and this?" One of the words the General himself could hardly read or remember. But he finally rapped it out impatiently, flung into the saddle and trotted away.

"Our baggage wagon is already rolling, Jesse," said Lieutenant Kirkland, one of the aides, as he too mounted. "But you can catch a ride on something. We'll be at a farmhouse—man named Adams— ask somebody," and away he went, leaving Jesse with only the vaguest idea of his future course. That was the way the Army treated the telegraphers in the first two years of the war. Only gradually—and grudgingly, it seemed—did the War Department realize or admit their importance to the service, and take better care of them.

Jesse sent Porter's final dispatch to the commander, then added, "I am closing the office now."

"Wait!" came back. "The Commander has something more—is General Porter there yet?"

"No, he is gone."

"All right. 73;" and Jesse busied himself at preparing to depart; packed his little knapsack, cut the wire four or five yards from his instrument and coiled it around the key, knocked down his small tent and folded it up. Laden with these, he headed for the road, which lay a little to the left. Already it was beginning to be a-clatter with the hoofs of staff horses, carrying division and brigade commanders, galloping eastward. Jesse sat down by the roadside, waiting for some wagons to come along. The darkness was now beginning to fade into grey. He looked at his father's big old silver watch—sounded like somebody grinding coffee when he wound it—and saw that it was nearly half-past three.

Now some wagons came along and Jesse fell in alongside the first one. "Hey, can I ride with you?" he asked the driver. "I'm General Porter's telegrapher;" showing his instrument and wire.

"Where's the General?" demanded the driver.

"Gone ahead."

"Why ain't you with him?"

"He left me with some dispatches to send, and he and his staff rode on to the new headquarters. We operators don't have any horses; have to get around the best way we can."

"Well, git on, bub," invited the driver. "Funny way of doin' business, seems to me."

"Me, too," agreed Jesse as he reached the seat beside the man. "What outfit you with?"

"Ninth Pennsylvany, Seymour's brigade."

"What you loaded with?"

"Tents, mostly, and officers' baggage."

"Well, I guess my little tent won't add much to the load." He tossed it back of the seat. "Where are you headed for?"

"South of the Chickahominy River; swamp, I call it."

"All of you?"

"S'far as I know. All I heard was, all wagons south of the Chickahominy. There's prob'ly gointa be a battle on this side today, and they know they're gointa git licked, and they don't want us wagons underfoot, clutterin' up the roads if they hafta run, which they prob'ly will."

This gave Jesse food for thought. He had helped to string the telegraph wire, and he knew that it ran for four or five miles on this side of and parallel to the Chickahominy, before swerving southward, to cross the swamp. Even so, it might be a long way from General Porter's new headquarters . . . He found himself losing his thread of thought as his eyelids drooped and his chin sank on his chest. A terrific jolt as one wheel dropped into a mud-hole jerked him awake again.

"S'pose I could lie down or sit down on the canvas back there and have a nap?" he asked.

"Help yerself."

"But listen, will you be sure to wake me up before we start across the swamp? I've got to stay on this side and find General Porter again."

The man nodded. "All right," he said, casually, belaboring and cursing his mules. Jesse subsided into some sort of nook among the jumbled load, and was almost instantly asleep.

His hours of dreams which followed were conditioned by the so-called road over which he travelled. He was in collapsing houses, falling down stairways, falling down rocky slopes, in railroad cars off the rails and bouncing over the ties, in buildings being shattered by earthquakes. At last he awoke, lay peacefully for a moment, then suddenly sprang to attention as he realized that it was broad daylight and the sun was shining. He crawled forward, put a hand on the driver's shoulder and asked, "Where are we?"

The man started and looked around in surprise and embarrassment. "Well, I'll be durned!" he said. "I clean forgot you was aboard. I guess I've carried you apast your station."

"Have we crossed the Chickahominy?" asked Jesse in alarm.

"Yes, but 'taint fur back." He gestured towards the belt of trees behind them. "Mile or so, I reckon."

"But you promised to wake me!" protested Jesse, grabbing for his instrument and knapsack.

"Yeah, I know, but these mules and these roads—I jest clean forgot."

Jesse was conscious of a great emptiness inside him. "Got any hardtack?" he asked.

The driver reached behind the seat and produced four of the big crackers. Jesse was too vexed to thank him or bid him good-bye as he dropped off the wagon and started back alongside the road, munching on one of the biscuits. When he had passed that caravan and had the road to himself, he ran, but presently slowed up as he began passing another group of wagons. In between caravans, as he neared the river—it must have been two miles— he could now hear distant musketry firing; the Confederates were in close pursuit. The road forked, and he hesitated momentarily— wagons were coming by both roads—then chose one at random, and pushed on, dog trotting, which made it difficult to eat his crackers; into the swamp, where the way was muddy and full of black puddles, from which he was liberally splattered by hoofs and wheels. He came to a sluggish little river, though one could not tell definitely where it was—a network of bayous, with a corduroy bridge laid across it, only a little above the water level.

Wagons were still coming, and he had to share the bridge, but little wider than a wagon, with a confused and struggling six-mule team, goaded by a cursing, lashing driver. Snatching his feet away from peril under their hoofs, teetering on the very ends of the poles in the floor, he was bumped by the hip of one of the plunging mules, shoved off into the thick, black water. Desperately, he held his instrument above his head, and succeeded in saving it from submersion; but his knapsack wasn't so fortunate, and he lost the last two of his crackers. His feet were tangled in roots and masses of decaying-leafy muck; the teamsters paid him no heed as he struggled slowly forward, and finally emerged, a sorry spectacle—streaming, black-muddy higher than his waist and spattered from there to the crown of his hat, water squashing in his shoes. Hurrying from the thick belt of timber into a weedy field, he scanned the higher ground in front of him eagerly. Which way was the Adams farmhouse? And where was the telegraph line? To his left—westward, he could see the infantry and artillery in motion, ascending the higher ground, cavalry taking position in the flat between the high ground and the swamp.

The sound of firing over beyond the plateau and to the left was increasing in volume, and now the boom of cannon was mingled with it. He waded a swampy brook—every watercourse in this locality was a wriggling marsh—and struck a rough road, skirting the foot of the slope. A countryman, riding a plowhorse, was leading a gaunt cow by a rope, hurrying southeastward, away from the battlefield.

"Can you tell me where Adams's farmhouse is?" asked Jesse.

The man pointed up the slope. "Half a mile the nigh way, I reckon, but you'll have to go around—muddy branch to cross—but I see you been in the swamp a'ready, so 'twon't make no diff'ence —" He jerked the cow's rope, whacked his horse with a switch and went on.

Jesse splashed through the brook, noticing worriedly the increase in the battle-roar, the smell of powder. Among the scattering trees on the slope, he found, glory be!—the telegraph line crossing his way. Now to find the General . . . he forged on, over the remains of a rail fence, into some fields, undoubtedly the Adams farm, and saw the farmhouse, as he supposed, several

95

hundred yards away. He was starting towards it when he saw a horseman galloping across the field in front of him and recognized him as Lieutenant Monteith, of General Porter's staff.

"Hi! Lieutenant!" Jesse shouted, waving his arm.

The rider stared, slowed his horse, swerved and rode towards him, his eyes wide with astonishment.

"That you, Jesse?" he asked. "Where've you been?"

"Got lost," said Jesse briefly, and the lieutenant, with a significant glance at his bedraggled condition, forbore further questioning. There was no time for it, anyhow.

"Where you going?" demanded Jesse.

"Carrying message from General Porter to the Commander," replied Monteith. "With you missing, we've had to communicate by courier."

"Some day," said Jesse, bitterly, "maybe the Army'll find it worth while to give us operators some transportation."

"I agree with you," conceded Monteith.

"Well, listen, Lieutenant," said Jesse, "I've found the telegraph line back here a little ways. Let me cut in, and if it's still working I can get the message to the Commander and an answer in quick time."

Monteith did not hesitate. "That's the thing to do, I guess. Lead on, Jesse."

"But why are you coming from that direction?" Jesse was puzzled. "Isn't that the Adams house?" pointing to the one directly in front of him.

"Yes, but we've moved to another house," he swept an arm to westward, "almost on the firing line."

Jesse ran back to the telegraph line, shinned up a pole with the end of his wire and hooked it on. Coming down, he saw to it that the bare wire swung free of contact with the pole or the ground. With his instrument on a rock, he began calling, "Mc, Mc, Mc," the commander's call, impudently breaking in between sentences of other conversations on the wire. At length Caldwell demanded crossly, "134?" (Who are you?)

"Bunnell," was the startling reply. "I have a dispatch from General Porter."

Days later, Jesse heard from Caldwell how excited and pleased General McClellan was when his call came in. "Cut off all other communication," he ordered. "I don't know where that boy Bunnell's been, but he's a godsend now."

Already worrying over how he was to write the Commander's reply, Jesse began sending the dispatch, telling of fierce and persistent attacks by the enemy all along the curving front—

("Open my knapsack, Lieutenant," ordered Jesse as he clicked ahead, "and see if there's any dry paper. I fell in the swamp—")

"So far," the report went on, "they are being held everywhere and suffering heavy losses, though the pressure on me is great. I am outnumbered, perhaps two to one—"

("No dry paper," said Monteith, exhibiting a pulpy mass in the knapsack.)

"I believe Jackson has now joined them on my right. My line is being stretched to dangerous thinness to prevent flanking. I need reinforcements—"

("Guess I can write the answer on the back of General Porter's dispatch," said Jesse. "But I'll have to have something hard and smooth under it—")

"I asked for axes earlier in the day, to fell trees for breastworks, but they have not come, and it is getting late now . . . The note of reproach and pleading continued through a few more sentences, ending with reemphasis on the need for reinforcements.

Monteith proffered his leather wallet, and with it under his paper, Jesse wrote the Commander's reply. He promised reinforcement and the axes (both would have to travel several miles and that would take so long! so long!). How far was the operator from General Porter's headquarters? asked the Commander. Lieutenant Monteith supplied the answer, "About a mile."

"Additional to General Porter," came the order. "Detail ten or fifteen orderlies to carry dispatches to and from operator."

Jesse had noticed that Monteith had a canteen with him. If a courier should be wounded and began to lose blood, the thing he would want most would be water.

"May I have a drink, Lieutenant?" asked Jesse. "I haven't had a drop of water today."

"Certainly," said Monteith, handing over his canteen. "Take it all. There's a well at headquarters."

"And if you can send another canteen of water, and something to eat," said Jesse. "I've had just two crackers today. And some

97

paper, of course, and a little piece of smooth board or something to write on—and another pencil. This one's about gone."

"I'll see what I can do," said Monteith, and rode away.

At last! A tired young telegrapher had a moment of rest, after two strenuous days and nights. With a sigh, he leaned back against the pole, listening languidly to the clicking of other messages. But this breathing spell could not be really restful, for the thunder of battle, ever growing louder, would not let human nerves relax. He heard Caldwell transmitting the order to General Franklin to send a division to Porter's assistance; McClellan always over-cautious, was afraid to detach too many men from his force south of the river. The commander soon wanted to send another message to General Porter, but Jesse was forced to halt it because he had no paper. It occurred to him now that he must go up in the edge of the field, so that the next courier might find his way to the telegraph office. But he found that Monteith had stuck a rail upright in a pile of rails from the wrecked fence as a beacon, and thereafter, the couriers came directly to him. The next one brought paper, a stub of pencil, a small piece of cardboard, a canteen of water and some hardtack. "They got nothing else," he explained.

The message he brought was in general, more of the same—enemy pounding hard all along the line, hoped reinforcements were on the way. To this the Commander replied that he had detached Slocum's division of the Sixth Corps, and they were en route via the Woodbury Bridge over the Chickahominy. He was also sending the axes. But with the battle increasing in intensity Jesse wondered whether, by the time the axes arrived, the outnumbered bluecoats could find time or opportunity or spare the men to cut timber and build breastworks.

At 4 o'clock Slocum's division was trudging up the slope west of him. One after another, the three brigades passed into the field, and were distributed to vulnerable points. "I sent Bartlett to the extreme right," wired Porter, "where flanking is threatened. One of our batteries was captured there, but Sykes has retaken it."

"It's hot over there," said the courier who brought this, showing two bullet holes in his clothes; and Jesse could readily believe it, for bullets and solid shot were now singing through the air and striking trees around him. "If I stop sending," he told Caldwell, "you will know that a ball has hit the wire or an insulator or me."

He moved his position a few feet so that he might sit with his back to a tree which would be between him and the worst of the deadly hail, which was coming from several points of a curve. The tree was a little more than a foot in diameter, but that was something. He moved a rock against it for a seat, and held his instrument on his knee when sending.

Then came a courier whose face was drawn with pain, and whose right hand was bloody. The dispatch he carried was bloodspattered.

"Sorry about that," he said through pale lips, indicating a punctured, bloody sleeve. "Couldn't help it."

"You ought to go to the hospital," said Jesse.

"Gotta get back to headquarters first." Jesse tucked the answering message into his pocket, helped him onto his horse, and he rode away.

A little later a courier arrived on foot and with a sprained shoulder; his horse had been shot from under him not 200 yards from Jesse's post. Time passed, and there was such a delay between messages that Jesse had begun to wonder whether General Porter had been taken prisoner, when another came riding, grimfaced.

"Got two dispatches this time," he anounced. "No answer came to the last one the General sent, and I found the reason on the way over—about half way—Sergeant Grose's body—he was carrying the dispatch. Here's his message, and here's the one I brought. You can explain to the Commander."

The message carried by the slain courier asked for more reinforcement for the right wing, and to protect the withdrawal which General Porter now admitted was inevitable. Jesse rushed it with an explanation, and the Commander promised help. In a little while he sent word that French's and Meagher's brigades were on the way to the right wing via the Grapevine Bridge.

The day and the battle grew, if possible, hotter. Sweat ran in rivulets down Jesse's face and body as the sun moved to a point where there was no shade for him. Bullets sang and nipped the leaves, and a cannon ball hit the trunk of his tree, jarring his spine. Porter's news grew worse—batteries lost because horses were killed—the enemy had a foothold on the plateau . . . About

99

6:30 the two promised brigades slogged towards the front just east of Jesse's office and went into action. The sun sank towards the horizon, disappeared, and the news worsened—more cannon lost, men exhausted, guns fouled by continuous use, ammunition for some units running low. At dusk, General Porter and staff passed on their way to the south side. "Stay here a while," said one of the aides to Jesse. "Brigade commanders may want to communicate with General McClellan."

So Jesse, ravenously hungry and thirsty sat there while darkness fell, and the conflict which has passed into history as the Battle of Gaines's Mill, one of the hardest fought of the war, subsided, with Federal troops still holding a part of the low, blood-drenched plateau. Some Confederate division commanders, in fact, had despaired of success in the late afternoon. But a steady withdrawal of Union troops continued throughout the night, the last ones leaving after dawn, and destroying the Chickahominy bridges.

Jesse called headquarters twice to report that no one had asked him to send anything; in fact, he doubted that any of the generals knew where he was. It was about 11 o'clock when he wired, "I am closing my office," and received a curt "O.K." in reply. He climbed the pole, detached his wire, wound it around his instrument, and stumbled through the scattering woods to join an infantry regiment heading towards the Grapevine Bridge.

He learned later that he wasn't the only one who had been overtaken by sleep on that strenuous day. General Reynolds, division commander, exhausted, had fallen asleep in the woods in the very heat of battle, and had been rudely awakened to find his own men all gone and himself being taken prisoner by gray-coated Rebs.

VIII

Cracker-Box Operator

At half-past two on the morning of that hot Sunday, the 29th of June, an orderly grabbed the shoulder of Operator Hervey Nichols, temporarily attached to General Heintzelman's Third Corps, and shook him vigorously.

"Wake up, Nichols!" he said. "The General wants a telegram sent."

Hervey, flat on his back on the ground, sleeping the deep sleep of a seventeen-year-old who, for several nights past, had had only broken bits of a night's repose, gasped and grumbled, came awake slowly and crawled out of the little tent—just a tent-fly propped on a four-foot stick—which was the only shelter he had. He scrambled to his feet, stretched, yawned and swung his arms to force himself awake.

"Wonder how long this is going to keep up?" he said,

"Ask old Bob Lee," was the retort. "He don't give us any peace. Personally, I wish they had Joe Johnston back in command of the Rebs. This old man Lee is too persistent for my taste."

Hervey sat down just inside his "tent," found his bottle of lucifer matches, struck one—it burned with a pale flame and gave off a sulphurous smell—and lighted his candle which was stuck by its own melted paraffin alongside his telegraph instrument on a cracker box. He could hear a confused noise of men talking, officers barking orders, a clatter of hoofs and wheels, whips cracking, wagon-drivers yelling and cursing. He held out his hand for the dispatch.

"What's going on?" he asked.

"It looks bad," replied the man. "There's been a conference of Generals—just broke up—at the Commander's Headquarters at Dr. Trent's house, a mile or so north of here. We're in for some

101

more retreat." Hervey was ticking away at his message while he listened. "Mc is going to move his base," the story went on, "to the south side of the Peninsula, where we'll have deep-water access. He's moving his headquarters to Harrisons' Landing—fifteen mile, I guess. On his way already, and they're stringing a telegraph line to it. We've got a whale of a lot of munitions and stores here around Savage's Station, you know, and the Commander thinks we can't save 'em all." He paused a moment, and exclaimed, "Look there!"

Hervey rose and peered in the direction of his pointing finger. Off there to northward, a red glow arose and rapidly brightened until—although the fire was nearly two miles away, they could see bright tips of leaping flames and rolling smoke.

"That's Franklin's Corps, retreating," said the orderly, "burning stores and forage, this side of the Chickahominy; good food for man and beast, Nichols. Well, so be it."

He took himself off, and Hervey, having completed his sending, stretched himself on the ground and was fast asleep again in a minute. And so began the fifth day of the Seven Days' Battles.

It was more than an hour later when his own call, repeated several times, awoke him. It was characteristic of Army operators that they could sleep through the clicking of their keys as other messages passed over the wire, but their own call never failed to arouse them after a few repetitions. Hervey awoke to receive a message for General Heintzelman and to find that dawn, a hot, sultry dawn had come; the eastern sky was red with the glow of coming sunrise, and all the landscape around, thronged with men, mules and wagons, was beginning to be touched with pink. Near by Hervey's tent stood a battery of artillery with muzzles westward toward the enemy, and their men asleep under the guns. Savage's farmhouse, on a knoll beside the railroad station named for him, was a center of activity. Three short freight trains, their engines with steam up, stood or moved restlessly about on the little jerkwater railroad leading east from Richmond. From them, ammunition was being transferred as rapidly as possible to wagons; and from tent and unsheltered heaps, provisions and grain were being loaded into other wagons, all hurrying—if a loaded Army wagon could be said to hurry—southward as they got their cargo. But it was painfully evident that the wagons could carry only a part of the vast store of material there at Savage's.

The whole area around—apple orchard, peach orchard, garden, fields and woods—was thronged with troops in loose formation; "Far too many!" criticized General Heintzelman. Some were preparing breakfast, and the smell of coffee and frying meat filled the air. It was rather early, but Hervey's young appetite was keen, and he decided that he'd better scrabble some breakfast while he could. Fried sidemeat, hard tack and two mugs of black coffee gave him a good start for the day, but did not interfere with his taking another nap shortly afterward. Everybody, even generals, snatched these half hours or hours of sleep, sometimes in the midst of battle. They had to. The human body could not endure through night after day after sleepness night of nerve strain with no intervals of repose.

The day grew busier. The enemy were pressing nearer. About 9 in the morning, sounds of cannonading and musketry announced that the Second Corps, under brave old, white-haired, white-bearded General Sumner, then in the last few months of his life, was fighting a delaying action some two miles to westward, near Fair Oaks. The combat lasted for two hours, then slackened and both sides drew back, Sumner having accomplished his purpose.

Messages became more frequent. Harper Caldwell, Headquarters operator, with his battery jars and all in a covered wagon, was sending from the end of the line as it approached Harrisons Landing. This and that corps and division commander was warned to hold the enemy off until the materiel could be removed or destroyed, and until the troops could all get safely across White Oak Swamp, the next hurdle they had to cross to reach the James. There was one consolation; White Oak wasn't as bad as the Chickahominy.

Hervey had been moved a little farther back from the front. There had been another operator near by, Charlie Jacques, but he was moved away somewhere as one division and another plodded southward across the swamp. Hervey was pecking away on a message when—Zing! Boom-crash! A shell exploded directly in front of him—he saw only a split-momentary flash of red and then he was hurled backward, half-stunned, overwhelmed with earth and gravel.

Tall, gray-haired General Heintzelman ran to him, crying, "Are you hurt, Hervey?" knelt beside him and began to brush the earth and gravel from his face, calling to an aide, "Bring some water." Half-dazed and with his mouth, eyes and ears full of earth, Hervey could not reply at first; but presently he gasped, "I don't think so, sir—not bad . . . It's just the dirt . . . " He struggled to a sitting position. "Where's my key?"

"Find it," said the General to nearby soldiers. "It's a miracle that a shell fragment didn't get you—why, it did! Here's blood on your shirt. Get a surgeon," to an aide. "And we'd better move to that clump of pines. This position is too exposed."

"Just a scratch, sir!" protested Hervey as to the wound in his side, but the surgeon came and dressed it, anyhow. A soldier found the instrument nearby, one part of it slightly bent, but still usable; but there was not an inch of wire left attached to it, and though the men searched all over the vicinity, they could find no more wire.

"Not a smidgen," said a corporal, "except about three foot left hangin' to the line that runs to the Commander's headquarters. It's all that's left of your connection to that line that you was usin' when the shell busted." He pointed it out. "It's right by a pole.

"Shin up that pole and get it down," ordered an officer. "Don't cut the line; just detach the piece of wire from it—carefully."

When the yard of wire was brought to him, Hervey attached it to his instrument, and aided by a cup of coffee, sat a while longer to recover from the shock of his near-disaster. Heintzelman's corps was ordered to cross White Oak Swamp, through a territory where there was no telegraph line, so Hervey was left behind, "where, Heaven knows, you are badly needed," said the General, "if they can find some wire for you."

General Wilson, in charge of supply trains, presently said, "Nichols, I've just got to get in communication with Headquarters. Can you think of any way? Can't that line be cut?"

"I don't like to cut it, General," replied Hervey. "General Sumner may need it. And to loosen it from the insulators and let it hang down to the ground wouldn't do. We're using naked wire, you know, and everything it touched would interfere with trans- mission, which is bad enough as it is. And somebody'd be sure to run into it and break it in no time. Only thing I can think of is to pile up some cracker-boxes against a pole, so I can get on top of them and—"

"Sergeant!" bellowed General Wilson. "Have some men bring some of those cracker-boxes and stack them against that pole, so

104

the operator can get up there. Put three boxes on the bottom, then two on top of those, so as to make a firm foundation, then one box from there up."

"Some of 'em's got crackers in 'em, General," the Sergeant reminded him.

"Don't make any difference," roared the General, "we've got to have a telegrapher."

There were not enough men nearby to handle the boxes as rapidly as the General wanted them, so he carried some of them himself.

"Put the full boxes on the bottom of the stack," he ordered. "You can lift the empties to the upper tiers easier. Now, Nichols, do you think you can get up there? Help him up, men, he's been wounded."

Despite the help, the climb was painful to Hervey's wound, and it bled again. Once on top, he attached his bit of wire to the line, set his key and sheets of paper on the box, and with his left arm hooked around the top of the little pole, he began calling headquarters, "Mc, Mc, Mc."

When acknowledgement came and Hervey announced himself, the usual gruff demand greeted him, "Where U been?" He explained briefly, and from there on was busy. A fight with the enemy was imminent. Sumner and his corps had retired nearer to Savage's Station, where the jam was now being lessened as one division and then another moved southward. Fast and peremptory came the orders from Headquarters, "Destroy stores;" "Destroy munitions;" "Ordnance and ammunition must not be allowed to fall into enemy hands." . . . Firing to westward indicated that pickets were been driven in. It was now near 5 o'clock in the afternoon. The fires from the burning hay and feedstuffs increased in number and volume. A train partly loaded with ammunition started eastward, its locomotive wheels sliding and spinning in the effort to make a quick start. The three forward cars were already afire. The engineer, having opened the throttle wide, leaped off, and the doomed train clattered away towards the Chickahominy swamp, two miles distant, the bridge over which had been destroyed. Before it reached there, cartridges were popping from heat. Off the broken end of the bridge the train plunged and piled up, a flaming mass, in the muck. For an hour and more, a great pillar of flame and smoke, a humiliating spectacle, arose from the pyre, with cartridges and shells bursting, as in a weird, manless battle.

Behind it a real battle was now on. Five Confederate brigades, plus artillery, were pushing towards Savage's, and a half mile west of there a hot fight was raging. Hervey, feeling unpleasantly prominent up there on that telegraph pole (though only twelve feet from the ground), hoped that none of the Confederate artillery officers was using field glasses. Bullets, solid shot and shells sang in the air, and the smoke from the burning stores was thicker than that from the battle. Savage's dwelling was riddled. The third train of munitions was set afire where it stood, just west of the farmhouse, and after much popping and banging, one car and quickly another blew up with a thunderous roar which jarred the earth so that Hervey clutched his little pole with both arms, feeling his box tower totter under him. McClellan, the Supreme Commander, was too far away to direct the course of the fight, so the corps and division commanders on the spot managed themselves. Hervey's work consisted mostly of reports to headquarters from these men as to its progress, though anxious messages continued to come back as to the destruction of materiel and the holding off of the enemy until all forces could escape.

For more than two hours the battle raged hotly, in comparatively level, open terrain, with no entrenchments and no natural cover. Then it gradually slackened and the Confederates withdrew a little, though their gunners continued to take an occasional shot at the eastern landscape in general, apparently just to keep in practice. The troops remaining around the station began brewing coffee and frying side-meat for supper. The wounded were being brought back from the field and the surgeons were busy at their bloody work—often ruthless and dreadful now, in haste because darkness and retreat were pressing them on. The few brief months of war that Hervey had been through had somewhat accustomed him to the cries of men suffering without anaesthetic under the surgeon's knife, but they never ceased to draw all his nerves to concert pitch. His youthful appetite, however, asserted itself, a great hollowness inside, as the shadows grew longer.

"Any chance for some grub down there?" he called to a group who were eating near by.

"We're all outa porterhouse steak and ice cream," returned

one humorist; "but we kin give you a sowbelly sandwich; best we got."

"All right, let's have it," said Hervey; and presently a man climbed up to hand him two sandwiches, each consisting of a slice of fried pork between two big hardtack crackers. He came back a minute later with a mug of coffee.

As dusk fell, messages became harder to read, and finally one was passed up to Hervey which—what with bad writing and darkness—he couldn't decipher at all.

"Hey, it's so dark I can't see the writing," he complained. He scarcely knew whom to address down there, for troops were moving away so rapidly that the official personnel were frequently changing. General Sedgwick had been the topsawyer for a while, but he was gone now, and General "Baldy" Smith seemed to be the only general officer left.

"You'll have to have a lantern up there," said an officer. One was taken from a wagon, lighted and passed up to him. He set it on his box and proceeded with his work. But soon he noticed that the whizzing of shot and shell was coming nearer and growing more frequent.

"This lantern's making a fine target for the Johnny gunners," he remarked.

"Oh, they can't see to aim in the dark," comforted someone on the ground.

"Well, they're making a pretty good stagger at it," retorted Hervey. He didn't like to be sarcastic with officers, but he noticed that everybody on the ground was staying several yards away from his pole; evidently it wasn't considered a healthy neighborhood. And sure enough, presently a missile snicked a corner of one of his boxes as it went by, nearly shaking Hervey from his perch.

"Cut a piece of tarpaulin," ordered the officer's voice, "three or four feet square and pass it up to the operator, to mask his lantern with." But then there was considerable delay while they were trying to find a tarpaulin, and the deadly messengers kept singing by, seemingly nearer and nearer. And when they passed the piece of canvas up to him, he had no means of attaching it to anything, to hold it in place.

"It should have been a whole tarp," he said. "Then I could've draped it over me like a tent." And while he was fiddling with it,

107

trying to find a way to make it stay in place, the disaster happened; a solid shot hit his tower amidships with a terrific crash, even broke the slender pole, and the whole structure came down with a prolonged crash, a welter of splintered boxes and crumpled hardtack, Hervey and his key on top of it, while the lantern went flying yards away.

There was a chorus of "Are you hurt?" and "Did it hit you?" as shadowy figures gathered around him in the darkness.

"Only shot full of splinters!" he snapped. There *were* two or three splinters sticking him, it seemed, and his flesh wound was smarting infernally, and he was getting into a bad temper. "From here on," he announced, "I'm going to stay on the ground. Should have come down from there half an hour ago. Somebody cut that wire and bring me the end of it." He was giving orders like a general, and they were being obeyed. He attached the end of the wire to his instrument, and for another hour he sent or received an occasional message. Then General Smith said, "That'll be all that's necessary. Better get out of here while you can;" and Hervey notified Headquarters, "Closing my office."

"Wonder if I can catch a ride going south," he said.

"There's a battery just leaving over there," returned the General. "Morton," to an aid, "hurry over there and tell those fellows to wait for the telegrapher."

Hervey detached his instrument and ran to the battery. "May I ride with you fellows?" he asked the men on the seat of the caisson.

"If you can squeeze in," said one of them, ungraciously.

"Let me sit between you," begged Hervey, "for I'm short of sleep, and I'll go to sleep and fall off, sure, if I sit on the end." He had attached his instrument to himself by a short piece of wire bent through a buttonhole.

"What about us?" growled one of the men. "We're short of sleep too." But they let him squeeze in between them, and more than once snatched him back when he was about to fall forward out of his seat. And so, jolting and jerking over ruts and rocks and gullies, his head almost snapped from his shoulders, it seemed, at times, but sleeping through it all, Hervey journeyed southward towards Malvern Hill and the end of the Seven Days.

A characteristic incident of those early days of the war, when telegraphers had to look after themselves occurred during this retreat, which General McClellan dignifiedly called a change of base. Embree, an operator in General Morell's corps, had been left behind to maintain some contact, but his commander had ordered a Negro, a runaway slave who had been following the army, to deliver a horse and three days' rations to him for his trip to the James. But after waiting for several hours, the enemy were getting so near and it became evident that this dark messenger wasn't going to deliver the goods—in fact, he heard that the "contraband" had been seen making tracks in the other direction, horse and all—that Embree started to walk to Harrison's Landing. The artillery and wagon trains from his command were gone, so there was no chance for a ride. He had been doing a lot of night work lately, and he was fearfully tired, but he slogged along beside a marching column of infantry, his instrument and a little coil of wire hanging at his belt identifying him as an operator. As the miles slowly reeled off, he at last saw a nicely-saddled horse standing by the roadside, with its bridle flung over a low-hanging bough. He glanced quickly this way and that; there was no officer in sight. "By gosh, I'm going to borrow that horse, I don't care whose it is," he muttered. He managed to lift one aching leg over the saddle, but he had not settled himself in the stirrups when a big German officer popped up into view, seemingly from nowhere, and roared, "Hey, 'vat der hell you do mit mein horse?"

Embree flattened himself, slid out of the saddle and tried to melt unobtrusively into the column of marching men, but they had seen the episode, and showed their appreciation by shouts of laughter and soldier-wisecracks; "No harm in trying;" "We'd like to ride, too, Percy, but they won't let us;" "Who do you think you are? Look—even our captain has to walk;" "Why don't you telegraph yourself the rest of the way?" and so on. Red-faced, he bore the gibes with what equanimity he could muster. But his tired body became more important that his bruised spirit, and he finally had to lie down by the roadside for a nap before he could complete the weary miles to Harrison's Landing.

IX

Night Escape

"What's the latest, Steve?" asked Major Simms, as he and one of his captains, Haggens, of Company A in an Illinois regiment, entered the railroad station at Kenton, in northwestern Tennessee. It was the forenoon of a mid-December day in 1862.

"We can't hear anything from General Grant any more," said Stephen Robinson, the fourteen-year-old telegraph operator. "Forrest's cavalry have cut the telegraph lines south of Jackson. They're working this way, too."

The major armies in the west were comparatively quiet at the time; the Federal General Rosecrans and Confederate Bragg watching each other in middle Tennessee, and Grant in Mississippi, keeping an eye on several Confederate opponents. The daring Confederate cavalry leader, General Forrest, however, was raiding in devastating fashion in southwestern Tennessee, pushing up along the line of railroad from Mobile to Cairo, which had been held at various points by small Union garrisons. The telegraphers at every town were in Union army service. The last message that had come through from Grant had ordered the commanders at the various points to hold their posts at all hazards.

"That last dispatch of the General's was typical," fumed Major Simms to Captain Haggen. The major had been a small-town lawyer and politician in Illinois before the war. "Hold your post at all hazards, says he! I wonder what he thinks the remains of three companies, a hundred and eighty-seven men, all told, and some of them with the bellyache, could do against Forrest's cavalry. Steve, remember you're not supposed to be hearing this. Don't repeat it to anybody. Keep it tight under your hat."

"Yes, sir," said Stephen.

"Easy enough for the General to give orders," the Major went on, "sitting there safe in camp with thirty or forty thousand men around him. My hundred and eighty-seven men would look mighty noble and gallant, of course, defending our little beanpole stockade to the last man, but it strikes me they'd be a lot more useful alive and with guns in their hands than dead or starving in a Rebel prison. Stevie, I cannot too strongly impress upon you the importance of keeping this conversation strictly private and confidential. It would hurt me politically if it got out at home."

"Yes, sir," said Stephen. "When are you going to leave, sir?"

"Oh, I didn't say I was going to leave!" protested the Major. "Don't be telling that to anybody. I'll let you know when or if I decide to move—and we'll take you with us. But don't repeat this to anybody. And be sure to save your cipher and instrument."

"That's the first thing an operator thinks of, sir," Stephen reminded him. "I'll destroy the code—I have it pretty well memorized, anyhow—and save the key, if I can."

The two officers departed to their little stockade north of town, which the major spoke of so contemptuously, leaving Stephen to meditate that the major, though he was an awful windbag, really had some reason on his side, despite the fact that he talked too much. No doubt General Grant did not expect a small force like his, however, to hold out against overwhelming odds.

Stephen was the only person remaining in his depot, and he felt more and more alone, as the awesome, graycoated cavalry swept northward, destroying railroad bridges—all wooden, of course—and telegraph lines. There was a railroad agent at Trenton—or had been—but for several days past no train of any sort had been running because of the track destruction to southward. No tickets could be sold and no freight shipped, so the agent dropped into the depot only once in a while to hear the latest news.

On Friday, the 19th of December, Stephen heard Holdredge, the operator at Humboldt, notifying the regional military headquarters at Columbus, Kentucky (which was 40 miles north of Kenton) that the telegraph wire had been cut at 5 A.M. about ten miles south of Humboldt. Holdredge owned a small hotel beside the tracks at Humboldt, and had his telegraph office in the building. The Forrest troopers rode into town on the following morning, seized and burned the hotel. That same day they pushed eleven miles farther north, to Trenton. Just before dusk, Jim

111

Lyle, the operator, telegraphed to Cairo and Columbus, "Rebs in sight and the fun has commenced." He stayed in his office to the last, but just before the troopers entered, he threw all his papers and his two keys into the big cast-iron stove, where a roaring coal fire made short work of them. When the first soldier, a sergeant, entered the room, he glanced at the bare table and asked, "Where's your instrument?"

Lyle pointed silently to the stove where the keys were rapidly melting. The men cursed and cuffed him a bit and took him into custody.

Stephen had heard his last message just before a corporal from Major Simms's detachment came in and asked, "Any news?"

"Forrest has just taken Trenton," said Stephen. "I heard the operator there say the cavalry were in sight, and that was the last word."

The corporal whirled, bolted out of the depot and sped northward, running.

Stephen had some sixteen feet of very thin wire under his table, which he had been saving for an emergency. He now drew this forth, rolled it into a smaller coil and laid it conveniently near on the table.

"I reckon they won't be here tonight," he said to himself. He killed another hour of time, then replenished his fire, locked the office door and went out to his boarding place, half a block away, for his supper. Mr. and Mrs. Telfer, his hosts, kept their political opinions to themselves, but Stephen suspected that they leaned towards the South. Mrs. Telfer took a motherly interest in him, catered to his tastes in food and ministered to him when he had colds, but he guessed rightly that her interest was entirely personal. They were of course eager to hear what was going on.

"When d'you think they'll be here?" asked Mrs. Telfer, as if he had been in General Forrest's confidence.

"I can't tell," he explained. "Only thing I know is that the wire was cut off at Trenton an hour or more ago. I think maybe they'll stay there overnight."

"Law me, I shore do hate to see 'em come," exclaimed Mrs. Telfer. "Calvary are so rough! They jest don't care what they do."

"I'm going back to the office after supper," said Stephen, "to see if I can hear anything. I may stay late."

It was a dreary evening. For some reason, after a couple of

112

hours, Stephen blew out his oil lamp and sat by the light of the open stove door. After all, Trenton was only sixteen miles away.

It was lonesome waiting there, as the lights of the little town winked out, one by one, and total darkness reigned. He almost jumped out of his chair when his key clicked at a quarter to eleven. How comforting it was to hear the headquarters operator at Columbus calling! It was almost as if he had been right there in the room.

"Still on the job, Steve?" he joked.

"Yes, waiting to see if anything happens, but I think I'll go home. I believe they've bivouacked at Trenton for the night."

Columbus agreed with him, so Stephen banked his fire, detached his instrument and took it and his flat package of wire with him to his lodging. If Forrest came early next morning, he hoped to escape. The Telfers were in in bed when he arrived, but awake—as were probably all others in Kenton—and hearing him enter, Mr. Telfer called to ask if there was any news. They were all up early next morning, and Stephen was at his office early. He had scarcely arrived when Columbus asked, "Heard anything?"

"No," he replied. "I don't know where Forrest is, but he'll probably be here during the day."

"Well, save the cipher," admonished Headquarters.

"Don't worry, I'll save it," retorted Stephen.

Under a gloomy, lowering sky, the strain of waiting made the Sabbath stillness unusually oppressive. Stephen puttered around his little cubicle, picking things up and putting them down, staring out of the windows and seeing little, for the whole town, like himself, was in a state of nerves, many staying home in fear. Church bells rang for Sunday school, and he wondered how many children would show up. Presently, Eb Whitsitt, house-painter, drayman and general repair man, lounged in, and taking the extra chair, asked, "Hear anything from Gineral Forrest?"

"He hasn't said a word to me this morning," replied Stephen. He was glad to see Eb; he would have been glad to see anyone who would help him to pass the time, and dryly humorous Eb was particularly welcome.

"Sorta unfriendly, seems to me," commented Eb. "Ain't done nothin' to offend him, have you, Steve?"

"Nothing that I can think of," said Stephen.

"Gointa stay around here 'til he comes?"

113

"Wouldn't be polite to go away and leave nobody here to welcome him, would it?" Stephen was keeping up the jest, but Eb promptly shattered it.

"No, I reckon not," he drawled, "but seems like our friend Major Simms ain't so accomodatin'. I jest been out there, and him and his three companies are gone."

"Gone?" Stephen's amazement, even dismay, was evident.

"Yeh. Seems like the word from Trenton yestiddy evenin' sorta upset him. Him and his men lit out last night with their tails in the air like a flock of deer; so Bill Harris tells me. Bill lives right nigh the stockade. They took out up the road to Union City. Dunno whether they aimed to march all night or not."

Eb went on talking, but Stephen said little. Now he was really alone! He was trying to picture the scene when the troopers arrived; would he be able to save his key or not? . . . While he worried and Eb rambled on, a church bell rang again.

"Well, there's the first bell for preachin'," said Eb, consulting a silver watch about the size of a doughnut. "Cam'ellites ringin' five minutes ahead of time, as usual. I better step home and git into my Sunday clo'es, such as they are." He arose and looked down at Stephen—so small and frail and careworn-looking that Eb's heart was touched. Laying a big, knobby hand on the boy's shoulder, he said, "Don't let 'em ketch you, Stevie."

"I'll do my best," said Stephen. But when Eb had gone, he pondered the question, Why am I staying here? Why don't I go now? The answer seemed to lie in the unsolvable problem, What did Forrest have in mind? How far north was he going to venture? Columbus would like to know the developments up to the latest moment, and they were depending on Stephen to keep them informed. They had there no force adequate to meet Forrest's troopers in the field, but they could defend their own post, especially if they had the latest news from hour to hour, so that they could prepare and bring in nearby reinforcements. Who could tell? Maybe Forrest had decided to drive no farther northward than Trenton. Maybe that was why the day was waning without his appearing at Kenton. Still, that didn't seem like Nathan Bedford Forrest. He wasn't the man to stop and turn back forty miles short of the enemy. . . .

Anyhow, noon came with nothing happening, and the nerve-strain increased. Stephen made another negative report to Col-

114

umbus and went to his dinner, which was always a little late on Sunday, because of the Telfers' attendance at church. After dinner various townsmen, including Eb Whitsitt, of course, dropped into the depot to ask if the operator had heard anything; but he was as much puzzled as any of them by the lack of any news.

"Maybe they don't do any raidin' on Sunday," suggested one man.

"I never heard of soldiers observing Sunday," said Stephen.

"Stonewall Jackson does, so I hear," said the citizen.

"But N. B. Forrest isn't Stonewall Jackson," Stephen reminded him.

"Hasn't Forrest got a telegrapher?" was the next question.

"Of course not!" promptly denied another caller, a wiseacre, before Stephen could reply. "If he had, he'd a been trying to fool Steve Robinson here with bogus messages."

"He couldn't fool me," said Stephen.

"Why not?"

"Because we talk in a secret cipher; and if there is an operator with Forrest, he hasn't got the code."

The group fell silent at that. The cipher was an awesome thing to outsiders. But one little man finally cleared his throat and said, "Ye couldn't tell us how that cipher works, could ye, Steve?"

Eb Whitsitt's roar of laughter was a sufficient answer to the question; but Stephen replied courteously, "I'm sworn to keep it secret, Mr. Higgins."

One by one, the loiterers drifted away, and the dull, raw afternoon wore on. Again Columbus called, and Stephen replied, "All quiet. I can't understand it." When supper-time came— supper was always cold on Sunday at the Telfer table—he asked his hostess to put up a couple of sandwiches for him, as he was going right back to the depot. He had a feeling that this day's work wasn't over yet. Mrs. Telfer made the sandwiches, and added a wedge of mince pie.

Back in the depot, Stephen ate his lunch rapidly while preparing for what might happen. He had a small woolen shoulder-shawl of black, gray and white plaid, such as men wore in milder winter weather in those days, before the modern topcoat came into use. President Lincoln wore one frequently. Stephen laid this on the table, put his flat parcel of wire on it and detached his instrument from the table, ready to add it to the bundle if he had to flee; though still leaving the key attached to the outside line, so that he could talk to Columbus. It would be cold, escaping through the night without that shawl, but it seemed necessary. He blew out his oil lamp, added no fuel to the fire, and with his hat on finished his mince pie by the waning light from the open stove door.

The church bells rang for evening service. He faced towards the table, his finger touched the key—clicked it twice, and then— *What was that?*—Distant sounds—the clatter of hoofs—many hoofs—the voices of men shouting orders! His premonition had been all too true. With one swift jerk, he snatched the instrument loose from the line, and rolled it, with his spare wire, in his shawl. With the bundle under his arm and the cipher in his pocket, he shut the door of the telegraph office behind him, to cut off the faint light from the stove, strode through the waiting room in four long steps, opened the outer door, slipped through it and closed it as quickly as possible. The troopers had come fast; they were terribly near. Clinging close to the wall, he walked to the end of the little building which he hoped was farthest from the raiders —but it wasn't! They seemed to be coming from all directions. He walked along the end of the depot—where a street crossed— as if going somewhere and surprised by the appearance of the raiders, stopping to gape at the first one, who rode up to and almost over him, quickly followed by others. This foremost man sprang from the saddle and ran into the depot. Coming back quickly, he asked, "Hey, boy, where does the railroad agent live?"

"Over on the other side of town som'ers," replied Stephen, pitching his voice higher and more boyish in tone than normal.

"What's his name?"

The boy appeared to ponder a moment. "I think it's Mr. Elzey or somep'n like that."

"What're you doin' out at night?" another rider demanded, roughly.

"I'm on an errand for my mother," replied Stephen. (The trooper would have been surprised to know how far Stephen was from his home and mother.)

"Well, you better git home," said the man. "Youngsters like you oughta be in bed. It ain't safe for little boys on the streets tonight."

"Yes, sir," agreed Stephen.

116

"Git along now," ordered the cavalryman, and Stephen said, "Yes, sir," again and hurried across the tracks. The raiders seemed everywhere; but when he turned north at the first corner, he soon left them behind. After going a half block on that street, he began to run; veered over to the railroad track and dog-trotted along the path outside the tie ends. Of course one couldn't walk between the rails; it was too dark to see the ties, and one would stumble and fall at every step. And once outside of town, the path became uncertain, too, and full of pitfalls. If the night hadn't been so dark! Half running, he fell twice, once dropping his bundle, which came apart, and he grew panicky before his groping hands found his key and wire. Thereafter, he walked, though still with uncertain footing.

He had not taken the wagon road because it forded the streams, and he had no desire to wade through cold water tonight. He shivered from chill until his teeth chattered; he hoped it wasn't from fright, though there was no doubt that he was scared. He knew that Forrest would learn all about him in a few minutes, and though no mounted man would try to follow him along the railroad track, he felt sure that there were fellows in town who would gladly do it afoot if the raider so ordered. As a matter of fact, Forrest guessed without difficulty that Stephen intended to tap the wire and notify Columbus, but the General didn't care a snap of his finger for that; he would continue to raid as far north as he chose, regardless of what Columbus might think of it.

The sounds of hoofs and voices rapidly faded away as Stephen left the scattered lights of the little town behind him. Once he turned to look back at them regretfully; they had never looked so attractive as now, when he was plunging into the pitch-dark country. In the first mile, he saw an occasional lighted window in a farmhouse; after that, none. Farm folk had followed the chickens to bed; it seemed queer that they didn't know what was going on in town. Stumbling and staggering, occasionally falling again, he walked on as fast as he dared. He wanted to put several miles between him and Kenton before he tapped the line. Gosh, how dark it was! When he reached the first trestle over a creek, he was very near walking off the abutment into the gulch; but his eyes had become a little accustomed to the thick darkness by that time, and he heard the purling of the stream and became dimly aware of the void in front of him just in time to stop and get on the track. There he felt his way across with his feet, and then took to the sidepath again. There were some other small trestles to negotiate before he came to a longer one across a fork of the Obion River, some two miles farther on. Once he passed a group of three or four houses, all dark and silent; a flag-stop when the railroad was operating. And once he saw, far off to the right, a light, a mere pin-point like a tiny star, probably in a farmhouse where someone was ill. Once in a while he felt a single drop of rain from the heavy, low-lying clouds. If it really started raining in earnest, he was in for some real misery.

At last!—the Obion bridge! Slowly, carefully, feeling his way with his feet from tie to tie, he passed this hazard. And then, when he had walked another half hour or more, he saw the glow of the coals of some partly subsided campfires. He guessed immediately that this was the camp of which he had heard, of several families of Negroes from plantations in the vicinity and farther southward, who had succeeded in escaping while Federal troops were in the neighborhood, hoping to find a new life beyond the Ohio River. So far, the small detachments of Federal soldiers along the railroad had served to protect them; but the vanishing of these units and the coming of Forrest would put another face on the matter for them. Stephen halted opposite the nearest of the fires and called out, "Hello!"

As he did so, he was aware of a dark figure not far from the fire, no doubt a watchman. "Who dat?" this man demanded.

"Robinson, telegraph operator at Kenton," Stephen replied. "I think you ought to know that Forrest's cavalry took Kenton about seven o'clock this evening."

"Lawd a-mussy!" came fervently in chorus from the man and another who had suddenly appeared from somewhere. There was no one whom they feared quite as much as Forrest.

"I got out just as they were coming into town," explained Stephen, "and I've walked the track this far. Where is this? How far from Crockett?"

" 'Bout two mile."

"How many of you are there here?"

There was some hesitation over this. One voice said, "Three fo' dozen," another, "Fawty or mo'."

Stephen was thinking fast. "Wouldn't you like to go up to Headquarters at Columbus?" he asked.

"Yes, suh! Sho' would!" burst enthusiastically from the group, to which others were rapidly adding themselves.

"Well, I'm going to telegraph them and ask if they won't send an engine and some cars down after us. I can't promise they will, but I hope they will. If they can't, you folks'd better get out of here as fast as you can, because I think Forrest will probably be along here tomorrow. Now if some of you will come here and help me—"

They came readily. They accepted his story as genuine. Stephen unwound his wire, and asked for a boost up the nearest pole. Strong arms lifted him as high as their heads, and he climbed the rest of the way, attached his wire to the line and came down.

"One of you bring me a torch from that fire," he ordered, "so I can see how to attach the wire to my key."

This was quickly done, and Stephen attached the wire with nervous misgivings. He had never used this piece of fine wire before, and he wondered whether it would work. If it didn't, he was in for a still longer walk. It must be at least ten miles to Union City and he was already tired. . . .

It worked perfectly. But his bodily weariness and his nervousness over the unfamilair wire made his sending sound not quite as usual. Columbus was evidently a little suspicious of it, but finally inquired, "Who is that?"

"Steve Robinson," he replied. "Don't you know me, Joe?"

"U don't sound natural," was the reply. "Where are you?"

Stephen related his adventures in as few words as he could then added, "There are 40 or 50 Negro contrabands camped here, trying to work their way north. U wouldn't want Forrest to get them, would you?"

"Colonel will have to answer that," said Joe.

"Ask him if he won't send an engine and cars here to get them."

"Wait a minute," said Joe . . . his conference took three or four minutes instead of one. Finally he came back and said, "Colonel not eager to take on a lot more dependents here, but will have to do it, I guess. How will engineer know where to find you?"

"About two miles south of Crockett. Will have fire burning on east side of track."

"It will be two hours, maybe three, before train gets there. We

119

have one engine, but steam is slow. Will have to fire it up. U are nearly 35 miles away; an hour or more's run."

"Have Major Simms and his men arrived there?"

"No, they are at Union City. We'll pick them up, too."

"They will send an engine and some cars for us," Stephen told the group around him, amid exclamations of thanksgiving. "It may be two or three hours," he added. "They've got to fire up an engine—and it's a thirty mile run down here. Keep a little bonfire going, but don't build it up too big. Forrest might see the glow at Kenton. Everybody get ready to leave."

The hours dragged on—slowly, very slowly it seemed; so slowly that some wonder began to arise among the refugees whether there was really anything to this promise to come and take them away. But at last a distant rumble on the rails, and the spark of a headlight in the north brought a hallelujah chorus from the waiting crowd. Stephen, awakened from a nap by the fire, brought down his wire and instrument, just as the engine, with several boxcars behind it, slowed to a standstill amid the gay chatter of the happy "contrabands". The engine crew knew Stephen, of course, and he was invited to the cab for the ride back to Columbus. The refugees were packed into one box car, and some of the infantry at Union City into the others. The rest of the soldiers were already on their way to Columbus on foot. Major Simms took pains to avoid meeting Stephen, and Stephen was quite willing to do the same.

Forrest came up next day as Stephen had expected; burned the main Obion bridge and rode into Union City, but that was as far as he went. He was too wise to try a skirmish with the garrison at Columbus. He had accomplished his mission; had destroyed the bridges on a hundred miles of north-south railroad important to Union armies, so he turned back and detoured to destroy bridges on another line.

Stephen Robinson served through the war in the Mississippi Valley. In 1864 he was operator for General A. J. Smith, commander of the 16th Corps. In the autumn, while carrying a message from General Smith to General Grierson, through an area where there was no wire, he was hit by a shotgun charge fired by a civilian, and fifteen buckshot lodged in his body. In the spring of '65, Charlie Pearson, a sixteen-year-old telegrapher, saw him on a Mississippi steamboat, going north, recuperating from his injury, though he carried two of the buckshot in his body for the rest of his life. The war was over and he was not yet of age. In later years, he was manager of the Chicago Board of Trade.

X

A Telegrapher's Temptation

"I hear that Dr. Wright, who dressed your wound, is in trouble —bad trouble," said Richard O'Brien to his younger brother John one day in '63 when both were stationed at Norfolk.

"What's that?" asked John.

"He shot and killed Lieutenant Sanborn, who commanded that detachment of Negro soldiers that landed here yesterday. He's a hot-headed man, it seems, and he was furious because Sanborn marched those troops up Main Street—fairly beside himself with rage. Sanborn sassed him back pretty vigorously, you can depend on that, but didn't threaten him with a weapon, so it's said. So it's going to be hard to make a case of self-defense out of it."

"Dr. Wright has been arrested, I suppose?" said John.

"Yes."

John stared through a window unseeingly. "I'm awfully sorry," he said. "He seemed like such a nice man, and he was very kind to me."

"Yes, but hot-tempered," said Richard; "and they're terribly touchy on the race question down here, you know."

Army justice was swift and sure. The doctor was tried by court-martial a few days later, and sentenced to be hanged.

There was great excitement in Norfolk over the case. Scores of prominent citizens came to General Naglee, who was in command at the city, begging to have appeals forwarded to President Lincoln in behalf of Dr. Wright, a prominent and popular citizen. Others sent letters by mail. General Naglee delayed the execution until he could hear from the President. In a few days a note came from Mr. Lincoln, "Send the proceedings of the court-martial to me."

The General did so, and then ensued another interval of waiting. Finally one day, the paper came back, together with one of the sad notes which the war President hated to write. The gist of it was that he could not interfere in the case; the offense was too flagrant; the verdict must stand.

The prisoner was informed at once, and the date of his execution was set. The news quickly spread through the city, and that evening—a cold, rainy evening—a young woman came to the military prison and asked to see the doctor. "I am his daughter," she said. She was cloaked against the rain, and with a hood that covered her head and shaded her face. When she pushed it back a little, the officer in charge saw that the face was beautiful and stricken with grief.

"Certainly you may see him," said the lieutenant, and called a corporal to escort her to the prisoner's cell. An hour passed, and the corporal reentered the room. "Miss Wright is coming out, sir," he said. With hood pulled forward over her face, which was mostly hidden by a handkerchief pressed to her eyes as she sobbed convulsively but silently, she followed him. The lieutenant rose, but said nothing as the cloaked and hooded figure hurried through the room and out of the door. But outside, as it went down the steps, a sentry, by the light of the lantern over the door, caught sight of the feet of the figure.

"Hey! Them shoes are too big!" he exclaimed, seizing the arm of the supposed young woman. There was a brief struggle, but another soldier came to the aid of the first, and the attempt to escape was foiled. Dr. Wright was returned sadly to his cell.

The execution date was named as October 23rd. The appeals for clemency continued to pour in, and General Naglee, for humanity's sake, notified the War Department again, in the two days that remained, of the strong feeling in the prisoner's behalf. On the 22nd, the day before the fatal one, Washington remained coldly silent on the subject. That afternoon, a sergeant came into Richard O'Brien's telegraph office, saying, "Dick, here's a citizen wants to speak with you." Telegraphers not being enlisted in the military service, army men were apt to use little ceremony in dealing with them.

The citizen followed the petty officer closely and turned to see him go out. Saying, "I beg your pardon, Mr. O'Brien," he stepped to the door to watch the sergeant go along the hall and then, convinced that no one was near by, he closed the door, came back and sat down. He gave his name—it was that of one of the most prominent families in Norfolk. The Army kept it a secret ever afterward.

He was a middle-aged man whose fine, intelligent features were sad and deeply lined with care. He was cleanly shaved and neat, though threadbare in attire. His broadcloth coat was shiny at the seams, and the edges of his clean white collar and cuffs were frayed, though the loose threads had been carefully trimmed off. He had done his best to present a good appearance, but the poverty of the besieged South was all too evident.

"Mr. O'Brien," he said, "I should like to request that this interview be kept confidential, but I cannot expect you to promise that."

Richard did not know how to answer this, so kept silence. He guessed that the call had something to do with the case of Dr. Wright, so the visitor's next words were not unexpected. He leaned forward and said, "You haven't heard anything from Washington today about the case of Dr. Wright, have you?"

"No, sir," replied Richard.

The gentleman's eyes searched his face. "You wouldn't hold back any such message if it came, would you?"

"Certainly not!" exclaimed Richard with some heat. "General Naglee has kept the President informed by telegraph of the appeals for clemency, and neither he nor I would think of holding back any notice of a reprieve. If you'll think a moment, you'd see that we wouldn't dare suppress a Presidential message."

"No, no, you're right. I apologize," said the caller, humbly. He paused a moment, scanning Richard's face. "You are very young," he said, "to hold so responsible a position."

"All the army telegraphers are young," said Richard, smiling; "most of them younger than I am. I'm twenty-three, and that's quite elderly, compared to some. My brother John, who alternates with me, is fifteen, and he went into the service two years ago at thirteen."

The man shook his head in wonder. "I know that the armies in this war are mostly mere boys, but I did not realize that such technical and responsible positions were being held by boys. I'm sorry. Youth is apt to be hard, inflexible. It takes a lifetime of experience with sorrow and misfortune to teach a man pity, compassion." He held up a hand apologetically. "No reflection on you, Mr. O'Brien. I'm just speaking in general terms."

Richard couldn't imagine what he was driving at, but he remarked, "I don't think that's always true, Mr. M. Take my young brother, for example. If he were in President Lincoln's place at this moment, I almost believe he would pardon Dr. Wright. The Doctor dressed a slight wound for him a short time ago, and quite won the boy's heart."

"—As he does everyone's," added Mr. M. "I deeply regret that he and President Lincoln cannot meet, face to face. Here in the South, Mr. O'Brien, there is much sneering and execration of President Lincoln, but we have heard that he is a gentle and merciful man. It seems strange that he is so inflexible in the case of Dr. Wright."

"After all, it is a case of murder," Richard reminded him; "and the victim was an army officer."

"There you are!" the caller pounced upon this point. "Some of us think the Secretary of War may have influenced the President in this case. Secretary Stanton has the reputation of being hard, even a ruthless man."

"It could be possible," admitted Richard.

"The citizens of Norfolk are terribly concerned over this trouble of Dr. Wright's," Mr. M went on. "The Doctor is one of our finest citizens, and one of the best beloved; hot-headed at times, quick to anger, but quick to repent of it and suffer great remorse for it. He feels very deeply on—the subject—er—which caused his trouble with your Lieutenant Sanborn. He's quick-tempered, yes, and I'll admit that he was in the wrong in what he did—greatly in the wrong. But the Yank—Federal officer used some very, very offensive language to him—"

"Which doesn't justify murder in the eyes of the law," Richard interrupted; "and it seems that he had a pistol ready."

Mr. M. spread his hands apologetically. "In these troubled times, Mr. O'Brien," he said, "many of our best citizens, even the most peaceful men, feel it necessary to go armed, for self-defense. True, it opens the way for tragedies like this. When suddenly angered, we are all apt to do things which are deplorable; which we wish afterwards we could recall. But nobody could or would accuse Dr. Wright of being a brawler—a man who has done so much for everybody. He has given his services to everyone, black as well as white, without knowing whether he will ever be paid or not. There are thousands of dollars in fees which he never

125

has collected and never will collect. He will never go to law to collect a bill.

"It may seem rather ridiculous, to you, Mr. O'Brien, but we are sort of one large family here; we are nearly all kin to each other—all the gentlefolk, I mean, and many of the middle class. There may be communities where not much attention is paid to that sort of thing, but in a small Southern city like this, most of us become relatives, either by blood or marriage; we are nearly all cousins. Dr. Wright is particularly close kin to me; his grand-mother—but I won't bore you with genealogy. In the North you probably don't notice relationships any farther off than second cousins, but we trace it many times farther than that, and are always aware of it. It means much to us. And no one of us has ever—ever suffered the sort of death—to which your court-martial has condemned Dr. Wright."

His eyes were wet, and Richard was deeply moved, "But I don't see," he objected, "why you come to me with this matter. General Naglee is the man to—"

The caller shook his head. "We have been to General Naglee, I among the rest. He has assured us that he has done all he could, and I am inclined to believe him. My approach is different."

He leaned forward and lowered his voice. "Has it ever occurred to you, Mr. O'Brien, that at this very moment, President Lincoln may be writing a reprieve for Dr. Wright—or that it may happen at any hour? Tomorrow morning, as I understand it, my old friend and kinsman's life will be taken. Suppose a reprieve, a commutation of the sentence came ticking in through that instrument an hour or so too late. How would you feel?"

Richard shook his head. "Not likely, sir. In fact, it's practically impossible."

"But there's a chance that it may," persisted the gentleman. "Suppose," he leaned still nearer and lowered his voice almost to a whisper, "Suppose you were to *anticipate* such a message; suppose you were to write it as actually having come from Washington?"

Richard was stunned to silence for a moment. Then, "Forge it, you mean?" he exclaimed, his voice rising.

With consternation in his face, Mr. M., in a quick movement, put his fingers upon Richard's lips. "Not so loud! For God's sake, not so loud!" he begged, still in a hushed tone. "Let me tell you

126

what you would gain by it. You would be a rich man; you would be paid twenty thousand dollars—"

"Confederate money?" said Richard, derisively.

"*In gold!*" And as the full impact of it burst upon Richard, his head almost swam a little. Mr. M. saw the effect of it in his face and was encouraged.

"As it would be impossible for you to remain here," he continued hurriedly, "we would arrange for your escape. A half hour after Dr. Wright had been released—giving us time to get him out of town—you would walk out of the office. You telegraphers, being civilians, go outside the lines whenever you choose. We would meet you wherever you designate and spirit you away, inside the Confederate lines—just as we will Dr. Wright. You may remain in the Southern States, have the freedom of the Confederacy if you like, or we will send you to Europe on one of our best blockade runners."

"Those blockade runners are sometimes captured or sunk," Richard reminded him, "and then where would I be?"

"You know as well as I do, Mr. O'Brien," said Mr. M., "that they are not often captured. "Some of them come in and go out almost at will. We will send you by one of these fastest ones, with the smartest captain. Think of being in Europe with twenty thousand dollars in gold in your pocket! You might not make that much in America in a lifetime."

"What assurance have I that I would get the money?" asked Richard.

"Only the word of a Virginia gentleman," said the caller, rather haughtily. "But I assure you it is a word that has never been broken."

While he was talking, visions of himself in Europe, a care-free idler, London, Paris, Rome, Vienna—with twenty thousand dollars to spend as he liked—and all for a few touches on that key at his elbow—flitted through Richard's brain; but then he saw the other side of the picture, too, and though it was with a slight tinge of regret that he saw that twenty thousand slipping through his fingers, he was not greatly tempted. He shook his head.

"I'm sorry," he added, "but I cannot consider your proposition."

"Twenty thousand is all we can possibly raise," said Mr. M.; "in gold, that is; and that strains our resources to the utmost."

"The amount doesn't matter," said Richard.

Mr. M.'s face was a study of disappointment and grief. "I'm afraid I'm not a very good bargainer," he said. "I've never tried to bribe anyone before."

"That doesn't matter, either," said Richard. "No one else could have done more than you have. It would be the money that talks. It just wouldn't work, Mr. M."

"It is an humiliating thing," said Mr. M., "for one of my family to attempt bribery. I hope you will understand, Mr. O'Brien, that it only proves our desperation, our love for our fellow-citizen and kinsman, our willingness to go to any extremity to save him."

"Mr. M.," said Richard, "it has occurred to me while I've been talking to you that if I were on your side, if I were in your place, I might be doing the very same thing you are doing."

"You are a very understanding young man," exclaimed Mr. M. with a startled look.

"And if you were in my place," Richard finished, "I am sure you would have given the same answer that I have given you."

Mr. M. dropped his hands in a despairing gesture. "I can have no retort to that," he admitted. "Yes, this is what war does to us . . . drives us to such desperation that we must try to escape by fair means or foul . . . It is enlightening to put oneself in the other man's place . . . So there is no hope, I suppose . . ."

He arose. "Am I free to go?"

"So far as I am concerned," replied Richard.

"Thank you. You have been very considerate. I understand your position—and respect it." He leaned forward with an imploring look. "You will listen, up to the very last minute, for word from Washington," he begged.

"Yes, sir, I promise that. And my brother, who will be at the key tomorrow morning, will do it just as eagerly as I would."

Richard had risen, too, but neither of the two men offered his hand to the other; the tragic gulf between them was too deep. Mr. M. turned and went out of the room without another word; but Richard understood that it was not in anger or discourtesy; it was because he was too full of emotion to speak.

Richard hesitated over the question whether he would better tell General Naglee of the incident, but quickly decided that it must be done. There would be some wonderment over why a civilian called on him and had a secret conference—some of the conversation might have been overheard by a soldier outside the door—no, it must be told. So he strode into the General's office, and briefly told the story.

"Did you have him put under arrest?" asked the General.

"No, sir," replied Richard, looking squarely into the commander's eyes.

"Why not?"

"I imagined myself in his place. These people would do anything to save Dr. Wright, General, and so would we to save a man whom we love and respect that much. It was their last hope. Suppose—well, suppose you had been captured, General, and that seemed the last possible chance of saving you. Would you object to our trying it?"

It had more than once occurred to General Naglee that this young O'Brien took too many liberties, was rather too free with his opinions. But after all, he was not in the army, he was not subject to military discipline; and the general had to admit that he was a loyal, clear-thinking young man who could be depended on to be on the right side of the question.

"Perhaps it was the best way to treat him," admitted the commander. "These people may be impressed by our moderation; and they will certainly be better acquainted with the loyalty of our telegraph corps." He paused and pushed papers about on his desk. "I dislike this job of being a hangman," he said. "I'll wait tomorrow morning until we can hear from Washington. Then, if no reprieve comes, we can proceed with the verdict. Don't fail to notify me as quickly as possible of any message."

"My brother will be on in the morning," said Richard. "He won't waste a minute if any news comes."

John came on duty next morning already sunk in gloom. He knew it was almost hopeless to expect any good news, but he couldn't help hoping. The night operator at Fortress Monroe reported an unexpected complication.

"The Great Atlantic Cable has quit again," he said. "Been off two hours. They think the trouble's near the east shore; been working on it but haven't found the bust yet."

To explain his jesting reference to the cable, the Army's communication between Norfolk and Washington first crossed by cable under the wide mouth of the James River to Fortress Monroe, thence, as already related, across Chesapeake Bay to the Eastern Shore, and by land up to Washington via Wilmington.

The cable across the Bay, a remnant of the original Atlantic Cable of 1858, which was a failure, was poorly insulated, and it went out of condition now and then.

General Naglee hadn't yet reached his office, and when he arrived, John went in to inform him that "The cable across the Bay has been out of fix for nearly three hours, sir. I'll let you know the minute it's working again."

The General cast a quick glance at John's face. He knew of the boy's sympathy for Dr. Wright, but that he might be delaying the message was a momentary thought, instantly dismissed from the commandant's mind. John would know better than to try that.

"Very well," he said. "I will delay the—matter until the cable is repaired."

John went back to his key, and the time dragged on. Once he called Fortress Monroe to ask if there was any news from the cable; but there was none. An hour passed—an hour and a half—and then his key began clicking. Fortress Monroe was calling.

"That U, John?" said the operator; they never used cipher in their casual conversation with each other. "Just wanted to tell U the old clothes line is working again. Don't know for how long. Nothing startling from Washington. The Capitol is still there."

"I want to talk to DI (the War Department call) for a minute or two," said John.

"GA" (Go ahead), said FM. and John put through the call. When acknowledgement came, in the familiar fist of Homer Bates, John said, "General Naglee would like to know if there is any news in the case of Dr. Wright."

"What case is that?" was the query.

"The civilian who is condemned to die here today for the shooting of an Army lieutenant."

Then Bates remembered. "Oh, yes. Wait. Will see."

After a few moments' silence, he came back with the fateful word, "Nothing."

John gulped, went into General Naglee's office, and standing very straight and pale, said, "General, the cable is working again, and there is no word from Washington about Dr. Wright."

The General's eyes were sympathetic. "Thank you, John," he said. "Now we must do an unpleasant duty."

When John walked out of the room, tears were flowing down his cheeks.

XI

The Adventures of John Lonergan

At thirteen, John Lonergan became a telegraph messanger boy in his native Kansas. In the next few years he learned to work a key, and in 1860 at seventeen, he was operator and clerk for the Milwaukee and Prairie du Chien Railroad in Wisconsin. He signed up for Government service in the Sioux Indian War in Minnesota in 1862, but had little opportunity to take part. From there he went to take a Civil War post in the Army of the Cumberland. At first he was stationed in Kentucky, from which the armies of Generals Bragg and Buell had just cleared out in the fall of '62, after the Battle of Perryville, leaving only the small force of the Confederate Raider, General John H. Morgan, and some bands of guerillas, whose only loyalty was to themselves, to keep the inhabitants aware that there was a war in progress.

John was stationed briefly at Stanford and Crab Orchard, and at the latter hamlet, he had the comfort of spending his nights in a house and sleeping in a bed, which was welcome indeed, for winter had come on. His host was a widower named Pearson, who owned a Negro couple named Hiram and Keturah. Hiram attended the garden and cornpatch, the horse and cow stables, while Keturah was the cook and housekeeper and took care of the milk and butter, lowering both into the well just short of the water in summer-time to keep them cool. Mr. Pearson kept his beliefs and prejudices to himself, and allowed John to do the same.

Most small town and country folk in those times, both white and colored, arose at the first peep of dawn in order to put in a full day's work. One morning in December the small contingent of Federal troops stationed at Crab Orchard under a captain was at the moment investigating a rumor of guerilla activity in an adjoining county. That morning Hiram was at work in the stables, and Keturah was nursing the kitchen fire—much cooking was done in the fireplace then—when she heard a distant clatter of hoofs in swift motion, which gave her a hint of what was coming. Knowing that young Lonergan was vulnerable to capture by the Confederates, and aware of his dread of a southern prison, she ran and pounded on his door, calling, "Mist' John! Mist' John!" When he did not immediately respond, she rushed into the room, seized an arm and started to drag him out of bed. "Mist' John," she exclaimed in a loud whisper, "de Reb cavalry is comin'. Dey in de street right now. Run out de back do' and git under de hen-'ouse." It was the only hiding place she could think of in a moment's notice.

John, half awake and too groggy to do any thinking, dashed out of the back door in his cotton nightshirt, but clutching his tele-graph key—he even slept with that!—and rolled under the chicken house. The coop, with its back against a fence, stood on legs a foot and a half above the ground, and had a small, latched door in its front. Gosh, it was cold out there! Keturah, close behind the fugitive, rolled a nearby fifteen-inch log some six feet long under the edge of the coop in front of him, which she hoped would conceal him. Then she picked up a few sticks of wood and strolled back into the house, affecting great astonishment to find half a dozen bearded, flop-hatted, countrified fellows with pistol on hip, searching the place, jostling the householder about and de-manding to know where the telegraph skunk was.

Neither Pearson nor Keturah would admit having seen the boarder since last night. "I dunno where he went nor when," protested Pearson. "He was jest a boarder. I had to take him; the Yankees made me. I didn't have no choice. He musta got outa here plumb early."

"Where did that telegrapher go, nigger?" they asked.

"I dunno nothing 'bout no tele-whatchacallit," yarned Keturah. "Yassuh, dey was a young man livin' heah, an' I've seen him peckin' on a lil' ol' do-funny o' some kind, but I didn't see him dis mawnin' an' I dunno which way he went." She was lying on all counts. She knew very well what the young man was doing.

There was one circumstance which fooled the raiders; they saw no clothing tossed over chairs, after the manner of men when they go to bed. The fact was that John had been brought up by

132

his mother to hang up his clothing and stow his shoes in a closet when he undressed, and being a somewhat fastidious youth, the habit clung to him as he neared manhood. A jumble of clothing, some the owner's and some the boarder's, meant little to the marauders, and they profanely gave up the puzzle.

Meanwhile, three others had invaded the stable, where Hiram was pulling hay down from the loft by the light of a lantern, took the light from him and looked the horse over. "Spavined, swaybacked, rackabones," was the verdict of one. "Wouldn't have him as a gift. I better shoot him—git him outa his misery."

"No, don't do dat, colonel," pleaded Hiram. "He's de onliest hoss we got."

"No, shootin', Jim," warned another of the raiders. "We can't be makin' too much noise."

They took the lantern out to the smoke-house, and each filled a bag which he carried slung around his shoulders with hams and bacon. Some alarmed cackles from the hen-house next attracted attention. "Hey, we can use some o' these," they chuckled, thrusting their hands in and dragging out fowls by the legs to be tied to their saddle-bows. The log protected John from discovery, but he was surprised that the chattering of his teeth was not heard by the men, and he wondered whether it would be better to be captured or freeze to death.

The men were evidently fearful of being surprised by Federal troops, for they frequently muttered "Hurry!" "Hurry!" "Git movin'!" and finally came the command, "Le's go!" whereupon they hurried to the street and galloped away.

Then John was so stiff with cold that Keturah had to drag him from under the coop and help him into the kitchen, gibbering, "C-c-c-cold. C-c-c-cold!" through chattering teeth. Mr. Pearson was stamping about the kitchen, purple with fury at the loss of so much of his winter provender. " 'Od-rotted guerillas!" he raged. "Not Confederate soldiers. Some of One-Arm Berry's gang, I bet, dad-burn their lousy, stinkin' gizzards. I'd like to have 'em stood up before a wall and me with a shotgun in my hands. Here —here's some of your clothes. Take off that nightshirt and let Keturah wash it when she has time. It's all covered with trash from the hen'ouse."

They stripped it off him, leaving him as naked as Adam in Eden, but he was far too near freezing to be embarrassed. Pearson brought him some more of his clothes and ordered Keturah to prepare a pan of hot water, for him to wash his face and head in. "And get another pan of hot water and wash his feet," he added.

"Another minute," shivered John, his teeth clicking like casta-nets, "and I'd have had to surrender to those fellows or freeze to death."

"It's a good thing you didn't surrender," said Pearson, fixing him with a baleful stare. "They were guerrillas, Lonergan. You don't surrender to guerrillas. They haven't got any nice Libby Prisons to put people in. If they got their hands on you, they'd've just taken you out somewhere and shot you."

John came out of that episode with a touch of frostbite on feet and ears. During the following summer of '63, while the opposing generals, Bragg and Rosecrans, presented a perfect example of stationary campaigning, casually maneuvering their armies to little purpose in Tennessee, John was working along the Memphis & Charleston Railroad between Memphis and Chattanooga. It was difficult to keep a wire in operation along there, for the Rebs or somebody cut it about every other day.

One night John and another operator named Briggs were traveling eastward on a "wild" engine, intending to look for breaks in the wire early next morning in an area where they thought them likely to occurr. The engineer, a middle-aged man named Griscom, was tooling along at about twenty miles an hour —it was dangerous to run at high speeds on the flimsy, often repaired track—when a terrific explosion lifted the left side of the engine at a point where they crossed a little wooden culvert. Griscom instantly shut off steam, and the machine reeled back to the left again, into the pit made by the blast, tossing the riders about like dolls and ending in a tangle of legs and arms.

"Planted a bomb on us," growled the engineer in a guarded tone. "Everybody still here?"

The two operators assented, but Jud, the fireman, complained, "My leg's caught somehow."

"I think I broke a rib or two when I slammed against the John-son bar," said Griscom. "Either of you boys got a match?"

"I have," said John.

"Let's have it." The match was one of those primitive sulphur affairs of the period, which lighted slowly and burned wierdly. Griscom felt his way across the cab, and the match was struck.

134

But no sooner had it flared up than three or four musket shots rang out from the neighboring covert, the bullets hitting the cab structure or zinging through it—all but one. Jud gave a strangled gasp and his head fell back, while a red spot appeared on his temple. He had been shot through the brain.

"They got him," growled Griscom. He leaned over the stricken fireman and said in his ear, "Jud! Jud!" But there was no response. His ears were forever deafened. Griscom cursed fervently in an undertone.

"Nothing we can do for him," he whispered. "We'll just have to leave him here until tomorrow. If we lit another match, prob'ly one or two more of us would go, time they reloaded."

"What'll we do now?" asked Briggs.

"We'll have to take to our feet. There's some Ohio cavalry at Paint Rock Bridge—or was yesterday. Nearest people I know of that would be friendly."

"How far is that?"

"Three, four mile."

"Let's go," said John.

"Gettin' outa here is gointa be ticklish," warned the engineer, who because of his superior age, took upon himself all the directing. "I dunno how close they are, but I think they're keepin' their distance, because they don't know how many of us are here nor how heavily we're armed. But keep low and don't make a sound."

Slowly, very slowly and stealthily they crawled out of the cab, to the pathway at the right side of the track. (Most of the shots, they thought, had come from the left side.) It was high time they were making a getaway, for lightning was flashing behind them, in the west, and evidently a regular gully-washer of a storm was coming. At the spot of escape, however, the heavy, low-lying clouds made the darkness profound.

Griscom, veteran railroader that he was, regretted his inability to place red lights on their wreck as a warning to other trains, but there was nothing that could be done about it. Crouching low and sometimes feeling their way by holding to the tie-ends, they made a slow, tedious and hazardous progress along the path. At times there was practically no path, and they were in danger of sliding down a steep bank. Sometimes they were confronted with a gulf, where the track crossed a bridge. Not until

135

they considered themselves a hundred yards or more from the wreck did they relax or venture more than a muttered "dammit" when a slip or stumble threw a man on one knee. Meanwhile the storm crept up remorselessly behind them, the lightning flashes illuminating the landscape more and more brightly. They cowered at every one, expecting more bullets. Once after a flash, two shots did ring out and two missiles sang past them, but that was all. Then came the rain. A pitiless downpour which quickly soaked them to the skin. With water squashing in their shoes, they slogged on, sometimes along the side-path, slippery with mud, sometimes feeling their way with their feet along the ties, or literally crawling across a bridge. In such progress, they did well to cover a mile in an hour. One heavy shower, with its terrific lightning and thunder, followed hard upon another. Once the others heard Griscom mutter, "Poor Jud! He was a fine boy." Wet as a drowned rat and miserable, he still had time to think of the lost fireman back yonder.

They could find no building near the track in which to take shelter from the merciless downpour. Twice they saw dim lights in houses not far off, but they dared not go near them. Once they passed a small shack beside the track, but its door was fastened with a hasp, and they had no tool with which to break it open.

Finally, when they had been creeping along for an hour and a half, John asked, "How far did you say it was to Paint Rock bridge?"

"Two, three mile. Three mile would cover it."

"Well, if we haven't come fifteen miles already," asserted John, "I'm a Chinaman."

"All right, you're a Chinaman, then," snapped Griscom.

"How'll we know when we come to Paint Rock bridge," asked Briggs.

"Them Ohio troops will shoot at us."

"Pleasant prospect," grated John.

On they plodded, for what seemed more weary miles, until John declared that they must be nearing Chattanooga. At last there came the challenge, "Halt!"

"We have halted," said one of the trio.

"Who are you and how many?" The questioner was not far off.

"Three men, unarmed."

A flash of lightning revealed both groups—three Union soldiers and the refugees—to each other. They were no more than two hundred feet apart.

"What's that in your hand?" was the next question.

"Telegraph instrument."

"Your names?"

"Lonergan and Briggs."

"Advance, Lonergan and Briggs and let's see you, and remember, we've got our fingers on the triggers."

"My God, we're glad to see you," said Griscom, as they drew near the others. "You're politer than some other fellers we met tonight. They shot first, without ever sayin' howdy."

The Ohio soldiers knew the telegraphers by reputation. The situation was explained, and the bedraggled trio were given a tent for shelter.

"But no beds," warned their hosts. "We're sleeping on pine boughs ourselves."

"We'll be thankful for that," they were assured.

The three removed their shoes and a part of their wet clothing (it was a warm night) and lay down on the pine boughs and slept like the dead.

In 1864 Lonergan was with Sherman's army in the drive to the sea. Late in October he was serving under the valiant General Oliver O. Howard, who had lost his right arm at Fair Oaks, but had patriotically gone back into action as soon as he was able, and commanded a corps in the sweep through Georgia. Here the Yanks frequently tapped the Confederate wires. Once they cut in just back of General McLaws's headquarters and obtained some valuable information passing between him and General Hardee. This gave a Captain Bedford in Howard's corps what he considered a "great idea".

"Let's have some fun," he said to John. "Let's send a telegram to Hardee in General Howard's name, inviting him to Christmas dinner at Savannah. Maybe Hardee'll get a laugh out of it, and maybe he won't. I think they were in West Point together. Anyhow, who cares?"

John was dubious. "But what will General Howard think of it?"

"Oh, Howard won't care," asserted Bedford, airily. "It's just a joke. He'll have a laugh out of it, too. They're good friends. He'll think it's a good sell."

137

"But this will let the Rebs know that we're in on their wire," John protested.

"That's all right. We can cut in on 'em again anywhere, anytime." Bedford was something of a rattlebrain. "Come on, make it something like this;—

"Gen. Wm. J. Hardee, C.S.A.

My Dear General;—

I invite you to eat your Christmas dinner as my guest in Savannah. With sincere regards and good wishes,

Yours sincerely,
O. O. Howard."

"Is that an order?"

"It's an order."

Still with qualms, John ticked off the message. As might have been expected, it caused an immediate reaction in the Confederate quarters. The wiretap was located and eliminated. Bedford, like the fool he was, couldn't resist boasting and giggling over the exploit, and in a short time the news reached General Howard's ears. He called in John Lonergan forthwith.

"Lonergan," he stormed, "what's this about your sending an insolent dispatch to General Hardee in my name?"

"Captain Bedford ordered me to do it, sir," John defended, "I objected to doing it, but he not only insisted, but he ordered it; and as he was my superior, I had to do it."

"But why didn't you check with me before forging my name to an impertinent message to an old friend of mine?" demanded the angry Howard, striding to and fro with his empty sleeve clasped under his left arm, as was his habit in moments of excitement. "General Hardee is my good friend. I have a very high regard for him, and I wouldn't for the world have sent him this sneering message, implying tauntingly that we are going to be in Savannah by Christmas. I should have thought you would have better sense."

"I know I should have asked you, General," pleaded John. "But you were out of your quarters, and he was insisting that I send it at once, and I didn't realize that—"

"And furthermore, you revealed to the enemy that we had tapped their wires, and we lost that connection." It was evident

138

that General Howard was regretting that he never used profanity.

"Captain Bedford said we would tap their wires again any time," offered John, blushing at the weakness of his excuse.

"That was a smart remark!" jeered the angry General. "We need to keep in touch with them all the time. I'll break that fellow for this, as sure as his name's Bedford. He's through as an officer. I'll overlook this in your case, Lonergan, though it gives me a lower opinion of your intelligence than I've previosly had."

He was as good as his word. He not only demoted Bedford to non-com. status, but he sent a letter through the lines under flag of truce to General Hardee, explaining that the telegram of invitation was a crude joke perpetrated by an underling, and apologizing for it.

XII

The Army's Life Line

When General George B. McClellan in 1861 took over the Department of the Ohio, which included western Virginia, Ohio, Indiana, Illinois, and later, Missouri, he appointed Anson Stager to superintend for military purposes, all telegraph lines within his department, adding "his instructions will be strictly obeyed." By this he meant at the start that military messages superseded all others on the commercial lines. His position was an extremely delicate one. But when the armies began stringing their own wires, a whole new world was opened up to the brass tappers. The Government's own telegraph system grew like magic overnight.

The higher authorities in the Army quickly realized the value, even the necessity, of the telegraph, but it took some lesser officers a long time to realize its unique position. Those operators who were attached to the staffs of commanding generals incurred the jealousy of other officers of lesser degree because they were so close to the big chief, on such unconventional terms with him and knew secrets which in many cases were even kept from them, officers in the same command. The general's telegrapher and cipher expert was in fact a private secretary. Being a civilian he did not have to notice the general's entrance, nor salute when he met him outside. The general was apt to call him Sam or Charlie. Other officers at times tried to pump him for news, but usually failed. The thought that a mere civilian, sometimes just a broth of a boy, should have this intimacy with the commander and this privity to important secrets which were often denied to them was very mortifying, and the smaller among them vented their displeasure upon the telegrapher in various ways whenever convenient. This feeling, carried into the decades following the war, had much to do with the steady refusal of the Grand Army of the Republic to recognize the telegraphers as brothers-in-arms.

Thus telegraphers frequently suffered from the irritation, misunderstandings and cross-purposes of in-between officers, aggravated by their chronic dislike of civilian co-laborers. Line-builders and operators were sometimes threatened with shooting because they did not perform miracles. General Alvin P. Hovey, in command at Memphis in 1862, claimed the right to read telegrams passing between General Halleck, then in command in the West, and two generals in Arkansas—which of course involved the revelation of the cipher. The Memphis operator refused to let him see them, whereupon Hovey ordered him under arrest. When Halleck heard of this, which he quickly did, he came down on Hovey like a cartload of brick. "Release the operator at once!" he thundered. "He did perfectly right in disobeying your order."

As we have already noted, General Grant was one who always gave full credit to the wire boys. "No orders ever had to be given to install the telegraph," said he. The line men and/or operators, without orders from any military commander, carried it forward as soon as an army halted or went into bivouac, the operator appeared with the end of a wire in his hand; that wire which, as the Comte de Paris so poetically remarked in his history of the war, was "more precious than the thread of Ariadne in the labyrinth of American forests," and delighted the commander by presenting a telegraph office, perhaps mounted on a cracker box, at the end of the day's march. As the war went on, the commanders came to expect this as routine procedure.

General Sherman was an enthusiast for the telegraph. "It's value may be illustrated," he wrote, "by the perfect concert of action between the armies in Virgina and Georgia in 1864. Hardly a day intervened when General Grant did not know the exact state of facts with me, more than fifteen hundred miles away as the wires ran. On the field a thin insulated wire may be run on improvised stakes or from tree to tree five or six miles in a couple of hours; and I have seen operators so skilful that by cutting the wire they could receive the message with their tongues from a distant station." On one day in '64 Grant wired not only Sherman in Georgia, but Generals Crook in West Virginia, Sigel in the Valley and Butler on the James River and received answers from all before nightfall, which was something of an achievement in those days.

At times of high tension, Lincoln, Stanton and Halleck might all be sitting in the telegraph room of the War Office, absorbing the news that came over the wires and occasionally making a suggestion which was not always committed to the wires, especially after Grant came in.

As soon as a large army halted or went into bivouac for the night, wires were strung connecting all corps and division headquarters with that of the commander-in-chief. The battery wagon which appeared in the Army of the Potomac in 1864, carrying the jars of acid and the chief cipher operator, became the rendezvous of all who, under any pretext, could lounge around there to snitch an earful of news. Even newspaper correspondents familiarized themselves with the Morse clicks until they could gather some tatters of news, occasionally stealing an army secret from a message which was not in code. The operator here had the convenience of a table for his work and semi-protection from the weather. All was lovely save for the day when the mules ran away and banged the wagon up against a post, smashing battery jars and creating a general mess, to say nothing of almost running into the enemy's lines.

During 1862 we are told that nearly 9,000 miles of wire were strung in territory occupied by the Union forces. Of this, nearly half was taken down or abandoned, as the necessities of the conflict seemed to dictate. As much more was strung in '63, and 1,500 miles abandoned; and thence to the end another 5,000 or 6,000 miles were looped across the landscape. They soon learned to use a mule for the wire-stringing, the reel of wire being mounted in a kind of sawbuck on its back, as it was led in a walk or trot, with the wire unreeling.

In 1863 a wire was even run down the Mississippi River into its delta and to South Pass, one of its mouths, 110 miles below New Orleans. A lonelier job than that of the operator cannot be imagined. All he had to do was to watch ships coming in from the Gulf and at least guess as to their character for report to his superiors upriver. Sometimes the operator was a man, rarely a teen-ager, and they changed frequently, lest insanity result from the loneliness. As it was, the operator spent much time in talking to the next station, just to fill in the dreary hours.

It was rare indeed in the East when the telegraph did not reach the front with the first troops in a campaign. An unusual instance was that of Gettysburg when Union and Confederate

142

forces suddenly clashed north of the town before General Meade, the Union commander, was aware that the battle had begun. The Federal wirehead had not been able to keep up with the advanced troops racing to head off the Confedarte hordes.

In the West the conditions were more difficult and the line-stringing was slower. Luke O'Reilly was operator with General Samuel H. Curtis when he advanced down through Missouri, but was not able to keep up with him, and was still ten miles distant when the Battle of Pea Ridge was fought, March 7th-8th, 1862. But Luke was in such high favor with the general that Curtis put him on his staff with the rank of second lieutenant and aide-de-camp. He continued to handle his job so admirably that later he was made captain and aide-de-camp on the staff of General Alfred H. Terry. These generals must have succeeded in wangling a salary commensurate with his rank for him, for legally he had no actual military rating with the War Department.

The telegraph followed General Buell to the Battle of Shiloh, thence to Bowling Green and Perryville; it followed Halleck and Rosecrans to Corinth. Grant directed the advance on Vicksburg by telegraph, and in December, 1862, heard with a stony face the bad news of the loss of his immense stores at Holly Springs to Van Dorn, the Confederate raider. He had a cipher operator, Beckwith, who was so necessary to the general that he went east with him early in '64, to share the top wire position in the Army of the Potomac with A. Harper Caldwell, who had served under Mc-Clellan, Burnside, Hooker and Meade.

Wire-tapping was a hazardous adventure, for it was liable to the death penalty. Strangely enough, this writer has found only one such where the ultimate penalty was inflicted, that of an unfortunate boy named Dodd, a Confederate operator who was caught by the Federals in Arkansas with some notes which he had picked off Union wires and was ruthlessly hanged at Little Rock.

Federal wire-tapping was usually more successful than Confederate, for 90 per cent of the Union messages were enciphered. A remarkable job of real spying was done by two Union operators for Rosecrans, Pat Mullarkey and Frank Valkenburg, inside the Confederate lines between Chattanooga and Knoxville in 1863. East Tennessee was largely Union in sympathy, and the spies were aided and fed by the country folk as they cut in on the wires along the railroad and listened to Confederate military information, which was seldom in cipher. The Reb authorities were aware that there was a bad "ground" somewhere, and searched diligently for the marauders, but for thirty-three days Pat and Frank eluded them, finally falling in with Union pickets, gaunt and with clothing and shoes in rags.

A Confederate operator tapped the wire between Washington and Burnside's army late in '62, and listened in until Union operators, suspecting his presence, advised him to "clear out".

The Confederate General John H. Morgan, famous raider in the mid-West, had always with him an operator named Ellsworth, who was a demon at stealing information from the wires, and who could imitate the sending of any operator he ever heard so closely as to deceive that op's best friends.

A noteworthy job of wire-tapping was that of C. A. Gaston, General Lee's operator, who entered the Union lines at City Point, Virginia, while Grant was besieging Richmond and Petersburg, and for six weeks listened to messages passing over Grant's wires. Most of them he could not read, but one, not in cipher, which told of the coming of a herd of 2,586 beef cattle, for the Union army, when sent by Gaston's courier disguised as a countryman, to Lee's headquarters, resulted in the capture of the whole herd by Wade Hampton's gray-coated cavalry.

W. K. Smith, General Crook's operator, once cut in on a wire in the Shenandoah Valley. When the Reb operator at Dublin heard his "ground," he called "Sign," but Smith, not knowing the Dublin call, disconnected. An hour later he tried softly to cut in again, but the alert Dublin man promptly challenged, "Oh, we know you're there, Smith, you damn Yankee." Smith laughed and admitted his interference, and the two joked with each other for a few minutes. When Crook captured Dublin a few days later, the operator had fled, but left a request with the railroad agent to treat his friend Smith courteously.

Union operator Foster tapped enemy wires between Charleston and Savannah in '64 and for two days copied messages which revealed a coming enemy attack on islands occupied by the Union General Terry. He relayed the news to Terry by a trusty Negro courier. Foster sank to his armpits in a swamp, was captured, and died in prison.

XIII

The President and the Operators

Charlie Tinker in his teens was happy in his job as telegraph operator in the lobby of the Tazewell House in Pekin, Illinois, in the 1850's. That hotel was a local headquarters for the circuit-riding judges and lawyers in their swings on horseback over their mud-bespattered rounds through still backwoodsy Illinois. Their jokes and stories of odd and weird episodes in the law and in the rustic circuits supplied no end of interest for the young operator.

One day when Charlie was momentarily idle, a tall, lank, big-footed man in ill-fitting clothes approached him with a winning smile on his homely countenance and said, "Mr. Operator, you don't seem to be very busy at the moment. I wonder if you'd explain to me how that contraption works. I've sent and received telegraphs, of course, but I don't yet know how it was done."

"Well, sir," Charlie riplied. "I'll have to own up that it's still a mystery to me. I know what happens, but I don't know why it happens. Electricity is what makes it work; and I might as well tell you that I don't know what electricity is, and I don't know anybody that does."

"Close kin to lightning, eh?" asked the stranger, who, Charlie now guessed, was Abraham Lincoln.

"Yes, that's why people talk about sending messages 'by lightning'. The nearest the professors can come to giving it a name is to call it a fluid; and anybody knows its not a fluid."

"Of course not."

"Well, anyway, we have to make a battery to produce electricity —" he pointed out his battery jars under the table and told how they were made ready. "But why those batteries make electricity send something along the wire is another thing I don't know. I only know that it does. We make the letters with dots and dashes.

145

Now f'rinstance I'm sending a message to you." He turned to an idle key. "A is a dot and a dash, B a dash and three dots . . ." he went on through the visitor's name, tapping out the sounds as he did so, and marking the dots and dashes on paper. When he had finished, Mr. Lincoln took the paper and looked at it quizzically.

"So that's my signature, is it?" he joked. "I'll try putting it on a bank check and see what the teller says. Now I'd like to see you do it rapidly, as if you were actually sending a dispatch."

Charlie rattled it off at his best speed, and Lincoln shook his head in despair. "At that rate, how in the name of goodness you tell one letter from another is beyond me."

"Practice makes it easy," said Charlie. "We have worse tangles than that. Take the word 'chores', f'rinstance. All dots. C is two dots, space, one dot; then double space and H is four dots; double space again and O is dot, space, dot; another long space and R is dot, space and two dots; another double space and E is just one dot; long space again and S is three spaced dots." He placed them on paper as he spoke.

. . .   .

Mr. Lincoln threw up his hands. "I give up. Hereafter, my respect for gentlemen of the telegraph will be most profound."

A few years passed, the Civil War came on, and young Tinker entered Government service; at first operating in two or three places in Virginia, but soon shifting to the War Office. There he saw his Illinois pupil, now President, every day, but did not feel himself important enough to remind the harassed man of their former meeting. Meanwhile, he had changed somewhat in appearance in growing to a man's estate, so that Lincoln did not immediately recognize him.

One day the President was in the office with three or four other men, and began telling a reminiscence of Illinois. The attention of Charlie Tinker, who was working on some telegrams, was caught by the sound of the word "Pekin." There was a prominent attorney in Pekin whose name, much to his annoyance, the President couldn't recall. The man had been a judge; Mr. Lincoln described his personal appearance. "I can't imagine," he fretted, plowing his hair with his fingers, "why I can't remember that man's name. Ought to know it as well as I know my own."

146

Charlie Tinker spoke up. "I beg pardon, Mr. President. Is it Judge Puterbaugh you are trying to recall?"

"That's it! That's it!" almost shouted the President, as he whirled to look at the speaker. "Did you know him?"

"Yes, sir," replied Charlie. "I used to be the operator at the Tazewell House. I once had the honor of showing you how the telegraph works—"

"I remember!" exclaimed Mr. Lincoln, slapping his hands together. "I remember you now; Charlie Tinker, isn't it? What a pleasure to see you again," as they shook hands. "You've grown so I didn't know you." Thereafter, they had many do-you-remember sessions together.

Scarcely a day passed when Lincoln did not visit the War Department Telegraph Office at least once, perhaps twice—morning and evening. It was probably his favorite hideout. There he avoided many a boresome and wasted hour thrust on him by visitors who had nothing of importance to say or who wanted favors. Anybody and everybody could walk into the President's White House office in those days, unannounced. Not only his office, but the Executive Mansion itself was open to all. There was a doorkeeper, but not infrequently he strayed off somewhere and strangers, finding the front door open, came in and wandered around, even upstairs. That was the democratic idea of the White House in our earlier years. It was the people's house, and they had a right to see it.

Coming down the gravel path from the White House to the old War Department, perhaps with some letters and papers in his tall hat, Mr. Lincoln might on hot summer evenings, come in carpet slippers. In winter he wore one of the little plaid shoulder shawls such as men wore in those days. Entering the telegraph room, he would hang the shawl over the top of the door, which his height made it easy for him to do, greet the operators—who were Homer, Bert, Charlie, Willie and so on to him—and perhaps toss a quip such as that to a youthful op who was putting vitriol into a battery jar one morning, "Well, sonny, mixing up the juices, eh?" One tissue copy of every dispatch to the Secretary of War, Secretary of the Navy, General of the Army and President was put in a drawer in the cipher chief's desk, and the President would go through these, sometimes remarking as he reached the bottom, "Well, I guess that's all. I've gotten down to raisins."

The story back of this remark, as he related it to the opera-tors, was that of a little girl who was overfond of sweets. One day she ate a quantity of raisins and topped them off with about a pound of candy. Presently she began vomiting, and after this had continued for a while, the remains of raisins began to appear. "I guess I'll be better now, Mama," she said. "I've got down to the raisins."

There were a few happenings that didn't touch off a joke or a story from Mr. Lincoln. The report of a commander that his troops had "fought the enemy to a standstill" reminded him of two dogs that ran barking along opposite sides of a fence as if eager to get at each other, but when they came to an open gate-way, they ran off in opposite directions. When General Burnside was seesawing around in east Tennessee late in '63, the War Department lost track of him for two or three days. When finally a complaint came from him about supplies or transport or some-thing, the President was reminded of Sally Ward, back in Illinois, who had fourteen children. Whenever a wail was heard from cornfield or creek bottom, Sally would say, "Thank God, there's another one of my children that ain't dead yet."

It was Burnside, by the way, on that East Tennessee campaign who drew from Lincoln the only word of profanity that the staff ever heard from him. The side-whiskered major general was supposed to go to the assistance of Rosecrans, down around Chattanooga, when a message came from him, saying that he expected to be at Jonesboro on a certain day. Eagerly scanning a map, it appeared to the Chief Executive that Burnside was moving away from instead of towards Rosecrans. "Jonesboro! Jonesboro!" he muttered, testily. "Damn Jonesboro!" Seizing a piece of paper, he wrote a telegram, "If you are to do any good for Rosecrans, it will not do to waste time at Jonesboro."

It was here in the telegraph office that he could find at all times an undisturbed hour to write some of his important state papers. The Emancipation Proclamation and that immortal peroration of the second Inaugural Address—"With malice towards none, with charity for all"—were written in part in the telegraph office. He would sit at an unoccupied table or desk, staring out of a win-dow for a while, then write a few sentences and pause again. His height made many chairs rather small for him, and he frequently sat with one leg bent back, the knee almost or quite resting on

148

the floor. Once he sat down to write at an unoccupied table with an instrument on it, which presently began clicking. An operator thrust an arm over his shoulder to answer the call.

"Have I hunkered you out of your seat?" asked the President. The operator transferred the call to another table.

When he had written what he had in mind, he would put the sheets into a certain drawer, and everybody in the room understood that it was to be kept inviolate; none of the operators would have opened that drawer for any consideration.

One evening as he sat writing, he looked up and saw Secretary Stanton standing in the doorway, silently looking over the scene with his usual contemptuous stare. "Good-evening, Mars," said the President with a bow; which didn't even evoke a smile from the vinegary Secretary. Both he and Secretary Seward deplored Mr. Lincoln's "frivolity". When he was telling a humorous story, of which he had an endless store, if Seward was present, he sometimes rose and stalked out of the room. The President never gave any heed to these slights.

One day he and Seward came in from some stiff, formal affair where the President had evidently been much bored. He threw himself into a chair and blew out a long and fervent "Phe-e-ew!"

"By jings, Seward," he exclaimed. "We are here!"

"Where on earth, Mr. President," asked the formal, humorless, Seward, "did you get that uncouth expression?"

Lincoln was startled, but promptly answered, "Bad company." Then, turning to the operators he said, "I ask your pardon, young gentlemen, for swearing. My mother used to tell me that any exclamation that began with 'By' is swearing, but I forget her teaching. I promise you I won't do so any more."

But there was a twinkle in his eye and a quirk around the corners of his mouth that told the boys that inside him he was laughing at the stuffy Secretary and he didn't care if they knew it.

His comments on war were almost never venomous. The Confederates were to him "the other fellows," and his playful allusions to the two Confederate leaders as "Jeffy Davis" and "Bobby Lee" had no sting in them. William Bender Wilson, who was a War Department operator for a while, and later wrote a small book or two, reached voting age in 1864, the time of Lincoln's second election, and received permission to go home to Pennsylvania to vote. The President heard of it and quizzed

Wilson genially about his politics. Wilson admitted that he was a Democrat. As they parted the President said, "Well, be sure you vote for the right kind of Democrats."

Wilson recalled a characteristic incident of this many-sided Executive. He was sent to the White House one day, bearing an "urgent" message from Governor Oliver P. Morton of Indiana, an excitable person who was subject to "border skeers," as the President called the frequent rumors from the midwest about the activities of subversive organizations favoring the South. Mr. Lincoln said he would go back to the telegraph office with Wilson to send a message. He also took one of his young sons with him. As they left the building, the President picked up a round pebble from the path, and said, "I challenge you boys to a game of 'followings'. Choose your pebble and see if you can hit me or pass me." He then shot his pebble along the path with his thumb and finger, and his companions in turn followed with theirs. Again and again they shot, but the President was an easy winner. "It wasn't a fair test," he admitted. "My longer arms and longer fingers were too much for you."

He could not always speak jocularly of the news, which too often was bad. After great disasters such as Fredericksburg and Chancellorsville, his demeanor was as one stricken to the soul. At the time of those battles and Antietam, Gettysburg, Chickamauga, and the Wilderness, he lingered in the telegraph room late at night, reading each telegram eagerly but with face drawn with anxiety. One night during the fighting of Second Bull Run, when Jeb Stuart's cavalry rode around behind General Pope's army, cutting telegraph wires again and again, so that Washington did not hear directly from Pope for three days and could only guess at the meaning of the rumblings coming faintly from 25 and 30 miles away, the President remained at the telegraph office all night. Wire communications at the time of that battle became appallingly haphazard. Operators were isolated from their commanders and became independent scouts (one of them was killed), observing the movements of troops of both sides from cliffs and thickets, and wiring their own versions back to the War Office on the rare occasions when they could cut in on a line.

On that May evening when the word was confirmed that incompetent General Hooker and his Army of Potomac had staggered back across the Rapphannock in defeat from the field of

Chancellorsville, Stanton and General Halleck were with the President in his White House office for an hour or two. They left him about 9 p.m., only a secretary remaining across the hall, with the doors open. The secretary heard his chief pacing the floor to and fro—plod, plod, plod, plod,—turn and return—plod, plod, plod, plod—driven by the goad of the seemingly unanswerable question, What can we do now? Ten o'clock passed, then eleven and twelve, and still the pacing went on. Shortly after midnight, the secretary said good-night and departed. Next morning Mr. Lincoln was at the War Office at eight o'clock, pale, calm, and quietly cheerful though not humorous. He was saddened again after Antietam and Gettysburg because his generals did not follow up their advantage and crush the enemy. A famous telegram which he sent after Gettysburg read:

> "I would give much to be relieved of the impression that Meade, Couch, Smith, and all since the Battle of Gettysburg have striven only to get the enemy over the river without another fight. Please tell me if you know who was the one corps commander who was in favor of fighting in the council of war on Sunday night."

Charlie Tinker recalled an occasion when the President, harassed as always by the situation in the field, but trying to relieve his mind with a jest, sat down near him and read something aloud from a newspaper or magazine, probably by the humorist, "Orpheus C. Kerr"—making it comic by mispronunciations, putting accents in the wrong places, and otherwise burlesquing the language. He sat with chair leaning back against the wall, one foot on the chair rung, and the other long leg thrown over that knee with the foot in its white sock dangling in the air. Tinker, with tears in his eyes, was laughing so hard about it that he couldn't remember afterward what the piece was about.

There was one duty which the gentle President never neglected. No matter how deeply he was concerned over National and foreign affairs, over war without and treachery within, over the long and desperate struggle to find generals who could win battles, if he heard of a soldier about to be shot for falling asleep while on sentry duty, he demanded the facts and usually sent a telegram pardoning the unfortunate fellow. The operators remembered his coming over from the White House late at night more than once to send such a message. He would never let a man be executed for so innocent an offense. He regarded the punishment as excessive.

He was in and out of the telegraph room several times on that November day in 1864 when he was being elected for the second time—deeply interested, though apparently calm. When in the evening, news was received which strongly indicated his success, he said to Chandler with a sly grin, "I wish you would send that dispatch over to the Madam. I think she is more anxious about this affair than I am."

Stanton once got it into his flinty head that Major Tom Eckert, head of the telegraph room, had been neglecting his duty— than which there could scarcely have been a more erroneous idea —and demanded his resignation. Eckert, after vigorously defending himself, sat down in great anger, to write the demanded letter, when he felt an arm laid across his shoulders and a familiar voice saying, "Mr. Secretary, I think you must be mistaken about this young man neglecting his duty. I have had opportunity to observe him, and I think he has been very faithful, sometimes working all night." With Presidential backing, there was no further question about the security of Eckert's job. Displacing him would have been not only an injustice but a disaster. The time came when Stanton gave him unstinted praise and said, "I would not trade my cipher operators for the whole clerical force of the Government."

Slowly the long ordeal of war wore itself away. With the surrender at Appomattox, it seemed that happy days must be here again. The President was quite joyful, but not triumphant; he was never that. But how little time—only five days—elapsed between Appomattox and the crime which was to curse the Nation forever after. Mr. Lincoln paid a flying visit to Richmond, not forgetting, while there, to call at the home of his old friend, the Confederate General George Pickett, and now confronted the mighty problem of reconstruction. How differently it would have been worked out if he had lived!

On the afternoon of April 12th, he came into the office, and when Eckert offered him his desk and chair, he said, "No, no, thanks, Major; let me sit somewhere else—in that room, there. I want to write a little more than usual. Bert," to Chandler, "may I borrow your pen? I like the way it writes." He took the pen

152

and paper and retired into a small adjoining room, where he wrote for some time. The only thing now remembered which he wrote then was a long telegram to General Weitzel, then in command in Richmond, about the proposed convening of the Virginia Legislature. He strongly objected to this and said so in plain terms. It has been established that this was the last telegram he ever sent.

Late in the afternoon of the 14th, he was in the office again for a short time, exchanged greetings with the operators and departed. This was little more than three hours before the fatal shot that was fired at Ford's Theatre. Some of the operators' eyes were wet at the thought that they would never again see in life the homely, kindly countenance which had never been turned towards them in anger.

XIV

Towards the End

Some operators who made their mark in the East in the early campaigns of the way—Bunnell, Nichols and Jacques among the rest, were sent west in '63. Hervey Nichols was eliminated early. He was left alone at Holly Springs, Mississippi, when the Rebs captured Grant's vast hoard of stores there. An operator who was supposed to stay on the job, giving news, as the enemy approached, until the last feasible moment, then make his escape if he could, carrying his key with him. Nichols' last words were, "Good-bye, boys, Van Dorn is coming. Devil knows what will become of me"; and then in a few moments, "Here they are," and with a defiant click, he went out of circulation. He survived a stretch in prison, and lived in Denver in his latter days.

General Rosecrans, after doing little in the first eight months of 1863, finally moved down below Chattanooga, threatening the Confederate General Bragg, and first took up his quarters at Crawfish Springs, just over the line in Georgia. Charles A. Dana, one of the editors of the New York *Tribune,* was with his army in a peculiar role—as an "investigator" appointed by the War Department. Fancy how the generals must have liked that! They didn't care for civilians, anyhow, and to have one of them at their very elbows, watching their every move and reporting it to Washington, was a bit thick, as the English would say.

There were three telegraphers with the army—Jesse Bunnell and two others whose names are lost to us—and when, on September 18th, they established connection with Chattanooga and thence with Washington, Dana, who was talkative as a parrot, sent eleven telegrams to Secretary Stanton in one day. On that day Rosecrans moved his headquarters three or four miles northward to the log home of a widow named Mrs. Glenn, advising her to move into the next valley westward, as there'd probably be a battle right in front of her place in a day or two. She complained that she couldn't see what they wanted to come battlin' around there for; it didn't look to her like no good place to have a battle. But she hastily gathered up a few necessities, and was moved in an army wagon over the straggling Missionary Ridge into the Chattanooga Creek Valley.

And none too soon. Already there was skirmishing to eastward, and next morning, the 19th, the great Battle of Chickamauga opened in full fury. All day Washington was kept informed by telegraph of the course of events. The Union Army was slowly forced back, but it was not until the next day, the 20th, that its real disaster occurred. Through a confusion in orders, a gap was opened in the Union line, through which the enemy poured with the "rebel yell," spattering the Federal tatters this way and that, killing General Lytle, as he vainly tried to stay the storm. This was quite near the Widow Glenn's house, which Rosecrans found too hot for his taste, and he retreated to Chattanooga, though the telegraphers stayed behind. Even in that hour of disaster, a sturdy defense by that stout old warrior, George H. Thomas, saved the Union army from total wreck. The telegraphers kept sending such messages as they could get from other commanders until the Glenn house began to be shot to pieces, when they retreated northward with keys and tools and set up shop temporarily on a stump. Driven from there at last by a hail of missiles, they retreated again with the last of the troops after nightfall to the little village of Rossville, three miles from Chattanooga, where General Thomas had halted.

The Federal army command changed soon. Rosecrans passed out and after General Grant's brief sojourn through the fighting around Chattanooga, General Sherman took over. Bunnell went with him in his drive to Atlanta, but in the fighting around that city he was painfully injured and retired from service. In later years he established an electrical supply business in New York City which is still in existence.

When General Burnside, still a bit groggy from his shattering defeat at Fredericksburg in December, 1862, was sent to Cincinnati in the following March to keep an eye on Kentucky, Charlie Jacques, who had been operating at various commands in Virginia, was sent with him. Charlie had two men under him,

155

a rather heavy station for an eighteen-year-old youth, but such things never seemed to bother these young wire wizards.

In September came a message, ordering General Burnside to Knoxville, to aid in forcing the Confederate General Bragg out of Tennessee. General Rosecrans, coming from Nashville, was to be the other jaw of the pincers.

"Now we'll see some action, Charlie," said General Burnside. "You'll go with me, of course."

They moved down to Knoxville with a part of the 23rd Corps and took it over as a small Confederate force began coagulating in the vicinity. Burnside fought them off, and meanwhile his men were working feverishly to complete a ring of fortifications around the town. Just to make it more interesting for them, after the Battle of Chickamauga, Bragg detached the redoubtable General Longstreet with a division of men to go to Knoxville and take care of Burnside.

But Burnside had been reinforced, too, and the siege which ensued was a notable one. The Union works at the west jutted out in a 125-yard square with salients at the corners. General William P. Sanders was in command there, and the bastion was christened Fort Sanders after he was killed there on the rampart. Here Burnside plumped Jacques down and said, "Charlie, I want you to set up shop here and keep me informed of what goes on." A wire was strung from there to his own quarters farther east in the town, where he had another operator.

On November 17th, the fighting was furious. Assault followed desperate assault on the works, but they held firm. On the 18th, Charlie's reports to the General ran something like this; "They are attacking on the left . . . fighting hand to hand . . . troops so mixed we can't tell what is happening . . . Rebs fall back . . . they attack on the right . . . trying to outflank us, but make no progress . . . they attack the center . . . somebody is carried to the rear . . . it is Gen. Sanders . . . center holds firm." Twice the wire was shot in two, and the General's headquarters decided that the work had fallen, but not so. Jacques, creeping along the line, found the break and repaired it.

Despite the loss of General Sanders, the outthrust bastion stoutly resisted the constant hammering which continued for two weeks. At last, on December 1st to 3rd, Longstreet began moving his troops eastward. General Lee had ordered him back

156

to Virginia to build up his own force in anticipation of the coming of Grant to the Army of the Potomac, which brought on the devastating campaign of 1864. General Sherman visited the works at Knoxville on December 6th and pronounced them well-nigh impregnable.

Charlie Jacques had his clothes patched and was able to buy a new hat by reason of his raise in pay; for General Burnside brevetted him as captain for bravery—another of those telegraph appointments which didn't mean anything permanent; just a temporary raise in salary and a slight lift to the spirit; no chance for a pension later on or military honors when he died.

In the East, beginning in May, 1864, Grant's Wilderness campaign, in which day by day he pounded Lee slowly backward, was the most strenuous thirty days of the war and the beginning of the end. Telegraph operators were more numerous and active than ever. They had to change locations every day, and often several times a day. In the incessant fighting, wires were frequently cut and no one ever knew whether it was by missiles or by enemy sabotage. Ed Hall remembered how he and Edwards and Henderson used to toss up a coin to decide who should go out and find the break in the line. As he started out, the unlucky man would say, "If I stop a shell, send my things home." Once one of these searchers found a sag in the wire, borne down nearly to the ground by the body of a man lying across it. By that time they were using a line made of seven wires twisted together and dipped in rubber. Once when the Union front was driven back near Bethesda Church, the Johnnies grabbed several yards of the wire, rammed it into a cannon and fired it at them. As it came whing-whanging through the air until stopped by trees, one of the Union brass-pounders quipped, "Wonder why they didn't send an operator with it." "Dode Moreland, for example," added a comrade, mentioning an op recently taken prisoner. "Or the lineman, Bill Stevens," offered another. "Never did hear what became of him."

In the fierce fighting around Spotsylvania Courthouse, one of the operators, running for his life, lost his instrument. Thirty years later a Negro farmer in that area, plowing in his cornfield turned up the key; and oddly enough, the original owner was still alive to claim it.

The bloody slaughter of the Wilderness campaign gave way

157

to the siege of Richmond. Then, as the winter of '64-5 drew on, the conflict moved towards a finale. The gory blunder of the Crater at Petersburg was only a brief setback for Grant, but his siege of Richmond dragged on for eight months thereafter. Sherman took Savannah and moved rapidly up through the Carolinas. Farther west, the country was gradually subsiding into uneasy, fretful quietude.

As the dogwoods and violets of spring—that fateful spring of 1865—blossomed in Virginia and along the Potomac, the North was asking in agony, "Can those rebels hold out much longer?" Then, on April 3rd, when Billy Dealey was the operator at Fortress Monroe, a call to "DI" came from him to the War Office. Tom Laird, the operator on duty at the War Department, answered.

"Turn down for Richmond," said Dealey.

Laird sprang to attention at once. Richmond, eh? Billy meant to turn down the old-fashioned armature spring in the War Office, so that it would respond to the weaker current from the more distant office and thus make the signals clearer.

"Do you get me well?" asked Dealey.

"Yes, go ahead," said Laird.

"All right, here is the first message for you in four years from

'Richmond, Va., Apr. 3, 1865
'Hon. Edwin M. Stanton, Secy of War, Wash, D.C.
    'We took Richmond at 8:15 this morning. The city is
on fire in two places.
'G. Weitzel, Brig. Gen. Commdg.' "

When Laird heard the word "Richmond" for the second time, he leaped from his table and ran through the offices, shouting "Richmond! Richmond has fallen!" pausing at windows to yell the words to the street outside. He left his task to operator Willie Kettles, aged 15, who had been listening, and who took up the reception where he left off. Willie himself was so excited that he upset his ink bottle on his desk. Secretary Stanton ran into the room and heard the conclusion of the message. A crowd was gathering in the street, and Stanton picked up Willie, who was small for his years, and held him in the window, while the crowd cheered as if it had been he who had taken Richmond. It was Willie's one moment of glory; we never heard of him before or afterward.

Lee's surrender at Appomattox was less than a week away.

At the time of the surrender, Harper Caldwell was in Richmond, Dealey at Fortress Monroe, Gilmore was in Charleston, the O'Briens were in North Carolina, where they had just completed a wire line down the Cape Fear River to Fort Fisher, Lonergan and Jacques were there too with Sherman, Lynch was in West Virgina, Van Duzen in Mississippi, Clowry in Missouri, Fuller on the Gulf Coast; and all were instructed to restore regular wire service as quickly as possible. Caldwell went to New Orleans with General Sheridan just after the war's end and died there in 1866. He was buried in his home town of Zanesville, Ohio.

The long struggle was over. In that four years of conflict, some of the teen-agers had grown into young manhood; some were still under voting age. Of the 1,200 operators and linemen in the service, about one hundred lost their lives in one way and another. Some of them suffered for years afterwards from malaria contracted in swamps or scurvy from long incarceration in rebel prisons. Twenty-five or thirty years after the war, Comrade Andrew Carnegie was still taking care of some dozens of families of telegraphers slain or enfeebled in the service. Not having been actual soldiers, they were not eligible to join the great veterans' organization, the Grand Army of the Republic; so they held their own little reunions every year and had good fun at them. At one of these, amid great applause and cheers, Marion Kerner read his poetic tribute to the war telegrapher, which we have quoted.

Secretary Stanton once remarked that he wouldn't trade his cipher operators for all the rest of the government clerical staff combined. The War Department in general seems to have remained only mildly appreciative. But the Government did not let the telegraphers go entirely unrewarded. It presented to each of what it considered the ten topmost figures in the telegraph corps, few of whom had seen service in the field, nice silver watches worth perhaps five or ten dollars apiece!